HOW
TO
SAIL

HOW TO SAIL

a practical course in boat handling

Nicholas Dent

St. Martin's Press Inc.
New York

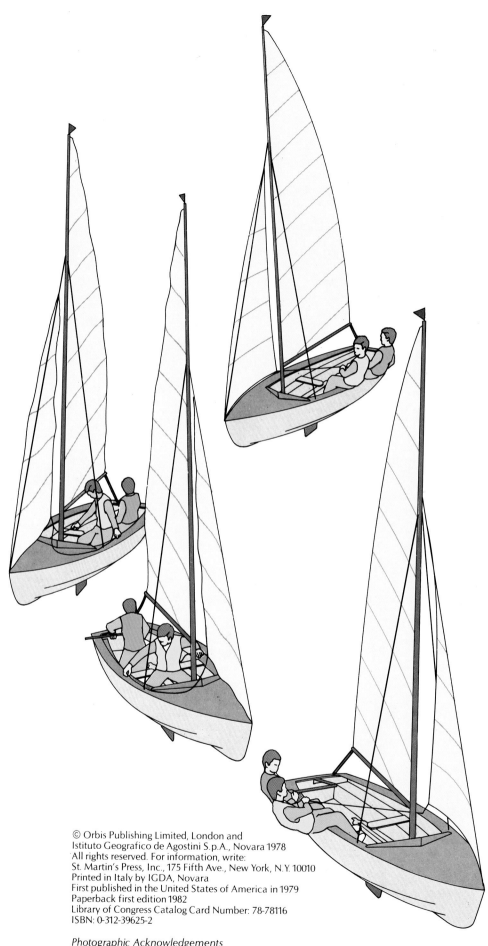

Printed in Italy by IGDA, Novara
First published in the United States of America in 1979
Paperback first edition 1982
Library of Congress Catalog Card Number: 78-78116
ISBN: 0-312-39625-2

Photographic Acknowledgements
Alistair Black: 8, 30, 32, 52, 63, 68, 98, 118; Patrick Blake:
Endpapers, 40; Gilbert le Cossec: 2–3; Bob Fisher: 51;
Radici: 80; John Watney: 16, 74, 108, 116; Yeldham-
Banks: 86, 105, 113.

Foreword

Boats and sailors come in all shapes and sizes – small and tall, wide and narrow, good and bad. Sailing has a serious side in which men dedicate their lives to the business of designing and testing new techniques for moving on water. And there is the hilarious side typified by the gin-and-tonic sailor, with peaked cap and reefer jacket, whose luxury cruiser never leaves harbour 'because the seaweed tells me we are in for a squall'.

Sailing literature, too, vies with its subject for variety. Adventure – Francis Chichester's *Lonely Sea and the Sky* – and achievement – Joshua Slocum's *Sailing Alone Around the World* – have been inspired by the world of boats. And now, taking its place as a must for any sailor's bookshelf, here is *How to Sail* by Nicholas Dent. If you have never sailed before, these pages provide a perfect introduction to the sport because Mr Dent assumes nothing, explains everything. If you have sailing experience, you will still enjoy the book – I have been a professional sailor for the last decade and I have learned much from Mr Dent.

My only complaint about *How to Sail* is that it was not written ten years ago. Armed with these instructional chapters and the very comprehensive glossary of terms, I would have been able to join in those mystifying yacht-club conversations and also handle a boat skilfully. Certainly it would have been easier than my own method of learning the sport – sailing alone non-stop round the world.

Chay Blyth

Contents

How to use this book

This is a complete course in sailing for the beginner, as well as the semi-experienced sailor who wants to become more skilled. To get the greatest benefit from the book (whether or not you have someone to instruct you) you should read it before you go sailing, and refer to it between practice sessions. When you have mastered the whole book you will then have acquired all the basic knowledge of an expert small boat sailor.

Each of the ten sections deals with one aspect of sailing. Sections 1 and 2 describe different types of sailing boat, what they consist of, and how they work. Sections 3 to 7 take you through the basic operations of handling a boat, both on the water and on land. Section 8 explains ways of making the boat sail faster and more efficiently. Special techniques for stronger winds are given in Section 9. Section 10 deals with the all-important matter of safety.

When you actually step into a boat you will need to use techniques from almost every part of the book. So it is important to read all the sections before you start (especially Section 10), with the possible exception of the parts dealing with more advanced techniques and theoretical considerations, which are marked by a red line across the top of the page. They are not essential for making a boat sail, but will set you on the path to becoming an expert.

Most of the drawings show the same two-person dinghy. This makes them easier to follow, but does not mean that the manoeuvres are not equally relevant to other types of boat (large and small), all of which are sailed by the same methods. The water has been 'removed' on most pages, so that you can see the positions of the rudder and centreboard at every stage. The blue arrows show the direction of the wind. It is very important to keep the wind direction in mind when studying the drawings on each page where the arrow appears.

The text contains only a small number of technical terms, which are explained as they occur. There is a Glossary of all the jargon of small boat sailing at the end of the book.

No one can learn to sail without spending time on the water, practising the techniques and manoeuvres. If there is an experienced sailor or instructor to help you, learning will be all the easier. But with this book you will also be able to teach yourself.

1. Sailing Boats

Sailing dinghies of several different classes taking part in a race. Normally these boats would race against others of the same class, but here they are racing against one another on a handicap basis. All these boats have retractable 'centreboards'

Although for many people sailing for pleasure is synonymous with yachting, the term 'yacht' is now generally reserved for larger boats which have a permanent keel attached to the bottom of the hull. As we shall see, a keel of some sort is an essential part of any sailing craft, but the vast majority of sailing boats in the world today have a retractable keel, or 'centreboard', which can be drawn up inside the boat when not required and are known as 'dinghies'.

Dinghies are small sailing boats, up to about 5 metres (16½ feet) in length, and have no cabin. They are relatively cheap to buy and the retractable centreboard makes it an easy matter to haul them out of the water at the end of a day's sailing. However, because of their small size they have to keep to more sheltered waters than the larger fixed-keel craft.

Most boats of both types belong to a 'class', that is to say, a group of boats all more or less identical in shape and size and usually displaying a distinctive symbol or letter on their sails. Classes normally exist to provide racing on equal terms for the boats in them. But the boats themselves are generally perfectly suitable for any type of sailing and many owners do no racing at all.

You can learn to sail in almost any kind of boat, but certain considerations make some boats more suitable than others. Dinghies are usually preferable, for example, to larger yachts because they are lighter and more manoeuvrable and you are much less likely to do any harm to yourself or others. At the same time, a highly sophisticated racing boat may prove rather a handful for the beginner because it will react quickly to any mishandling, before you have time to rectify your mistake. If the boat is too sluggish, on the other hand, it may be difficult to tell when you are doing something wrong.

The next few pages show some of the smaller types of sailing boat, including some that are suitable for the beginner and some for the more experienced sailor.

Boats for beginners

Modern two-person dinghy This is undoubtedly the most common type of sailing boat in the world and so it is the natural choice for many people when learning to sail. Two-person boats range in size from about 3 metres (10 feet) to 5 metres (16½ feet). The smaller ones are designed for children, while an ideal size for adult learners is between 3.5 metres (11½ feet) and 4 metres (13 feet). They may vary considerably in shape, layout and construction, but they almost invariably have two sails (sometimes with a spinnaker as an optional extra). The two crew members are known as the Helmsman, who steers the boat, and Crew. Modern dinghies are very light compared with older types and are easy to handle out of the water as well as on it. Some are built in plywood, but many are made of glass-fibre which has the advantage of requiring very little maintenance. The mast and boom are usually made of a lightweight aluminium alloy and almost all sails and fittings are made from synthetic materials which do not rot or rust. The average two-person dinghy is an excellent compromise between a racing and a cruising boat. It is roomy and stable enough for comfortable day cruises in sheltered waters, but fast and responsive enough for racing. Although they may not have all the sophisticated equipment of a thoroughbred racing boat, large fleets of these boats take part in races and regattas all over the world.

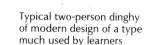

Typical two-person dinghy of modern design of a type much used by learners

Glass-fibre dinghy based on traditional craft, with room for several people on board

Three-person dinghy of traditional design, with clinker construction, a 'gaff' rig and short 'bowsprit'

Family dinghy As the name suggests, these boats can accommodate several people, six or seven in the larger ones which may be 5.5 metres (18 feet) in length. They are strictly cruising boats, but they are lively enough to teach a beginner the basic skills of sailing. The design is usually based on traditional small fishing craft, using modern building materials to combine the seaworthiness of the one with the ease of upkeep of the other.

Traditional dinghy The older style of dinghy tends to be rather heavier and slower than its modern counterpart, but it has greater character and often a good sailing performance. The hull is usually made of overlapping planks ('clinker' construction) which makes it very robust. A common feature is the 'gaff' rig which means that the mainsail has four edges, the highest one being attached to a gaff which is suspended near the top of the mast.

Pram dinghy More people have probably learned to sail in this type of boat than any other. With a length of only 2 metres (6½ feet), it is strictly for children and there is obviously no room on board for an accompanying adult. However, provided sensible precautions are taken, the young helmsman or helmswoman can come to little harm. The boat is safe and stable, and a six-year-old should have no difficulty in managing the small sail which is a miniature version of the one used on traditional sailing barges. When not in use, the mast and rigging can all be packed away inside the boat and the whole lot lifted onto the roof of a car. The simple lines, especially the distinctive truncated bow, make this an exceptionally easy boat to build at home. (In fact, the word 'pram' refers to the shape of the bow rather than the diminuitive size of the occupant.) All these advantages have made this one of the most numerous types of boat in the world and there are quite large fleets in many places. Races are held at many of these centres, giving the beginner a chance to learn the techniques of racing, as well as sailing, at an early age.

Small 'pram' dinghy, highly suitable for teaching a child to sail and race

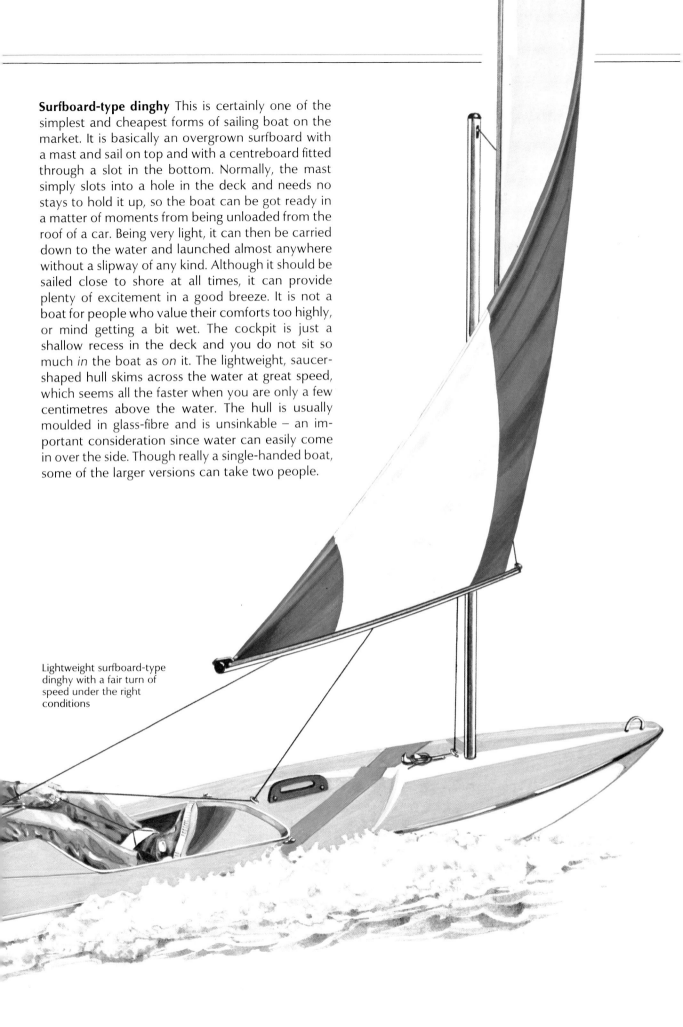

Surfboard-type dinghy This is certainly one of the simplest and cheapest forms of sailing boat on the market. It is basically an overgrown surfboard with a mast and sail on top and with a centreboard fitted through a slot in the bottom. Normally, the mast simply slots into a hole in the deck and needs no stays to hold it up, so the boat can be got ready in a matter of moments from being unloaded from the roof of a car. Being very light, it can then be carried down to the water and launched almost anywhere without a slipway of any kind. Although it should be sailed close to shore at all times, it can provide plenty of excitement in a good breeze. It is not a boat for people who value their comforts too highly, or mind getting a bit wet. The cockpit is just a shallow recess in the deck and you do not sit so much *in* the boat as *on* it. The lightweight, saucer-shaped hull skims across the water at great speed, which seems all the faster when you are only a few centimetres above the water. The hull is usually moulded in glass-fibre and is unsinkable – an important consideration since water can easily come in over the side. Though really a single-handed boat, some of the larger versions can take two people.

Lightweight surfboard-type dinghy with a fair turn of speed under the right conditions

Fast racing catamaran, capable of high speeds when handled by experts

Boats for the expert

Racing dinghy Racing dinghies are the thorough-breds of the dinghy world and tend to be faster and more responsive than boats which are designed for a less strenuous type of sailing. They also have more ropes, wires and other paraphernalia than you need simply to make the boat sail. Some of them are one-man boats; others are for two people. They may belong to any one of dozens of classes. In a few of these, known as 'development classes', the boats are not identical in design and individual designers can try and create the fastest possible boat within certain limitations laid down by the rules of the class, and this adds another dimension to the sport.

Sophisticated racing dinghy, demanding great skill from both Helmsman and Crew

Ocean racer To own an ocean racer is the dream of many sailors. Unfortunately, the cost of buying and running one is beyond the means of most private individuals, but an increasing number are owned collectively by groups of people of quite modest means. Ocean racers range in length from about 6 metres (19½ feet) to 20 metres (65½ feet) and more. Although they vary widely in shape as well as size, they can all race against one another on equal terms because of an elaborate system of handicapping, known as the International Offshore Rule. The first ocean racers were essentially cruising boats which raced occasionally. Many modern boats, on the other hand, are out-and-out racing 'machines', with the barest minimum of human comforts in their cabins in order to save weight and gain a little precious speed. However, other boats are fitted out as comfortable cruising vessels at the cost of a slight loss of speed when racing. These are often known as 'cruiser-racers'.

Medium-sized ocean racer, also suitable for comfortable cruising voyages

Catamaran Catamarans are the fastest sailing boats in existence. Some of them are capable of speeds of 50 kph (31 mph) and more. This is because the two widely-spaced, but narrow hulls create a boat which is, at the same time, both extremely stable and highly streamlined. Unfortunately, catamarans are relatively difficult to manoeuvre, especially in a confined space, and catamaran sailors have to learn some special techniques in addition to the normal skills of sailing. Therefore they are not recommended for the complete beginner. As well as catamarans, there are sailing boats with three hulls, known as 'trimarans', but these are usually larger boats, with cabins.

2. The Boat: A Sailing Machine

Interior of a modern dinghy. This boat is fully equipped for racing, and some of the equipment is used for coaxing the last ounce of speed from the wind. You would not need to use all the equipment if you were just starting to sail

A sailing boat is, first and foremost, a machine for turning the force of the wind into forward motion through the water. All the parts of the boat, such as rudder, centreboard, mast, rigging and sails, play a part in this process. In this section we will see how each of the components works on its own and then see how they work as a whole to enable the boat to make progress against the wind as well as with it.

The parts of the boat described on the following pages are all those which you need to know in order to prepare the boat and sail it. They may not always look exactly the same on every boat you see, but you should have little difficulty in identifying the ones which correspond to those which are illustrated. To help you, some of the more common variations have been shown too. As we have already noted, some boats, especially racing models, have a lot more paraphernalia than is necessary simply to make the boat sail along. Most of this has to do with 'tuning' the boat to obtain maximum speed in all different conditions of wind and sea. Some of these optional extras are described later in the book, but they are chiefly of interest to the competitive sailor and you can safely ignore them while you are learning.

Some dinghies, especially older ones, may have fewer fittings, in fact, than the one shown. For example, they may not have a tiller extension, kicking-strap or toestraps. In all probability, they can be managed quite easily without them and it should not be assumed that the boat is any the worse for not having them, especially if it is to be used for learning to sail.

It is perfectly possible to sail a boat without knowing exactly how it is able to make progress through the water, just as it is possible to drive a motor car without knowing how an internal combustion engine works. But, as with a car, knowing how your boat works can help you to get better performance from it and to diagnose faults if they occur. The fact that a boat is able to sail *against* the wind as well as *with* it is also fascinating enough in itself, so the last part of this section deals with how a boat works.

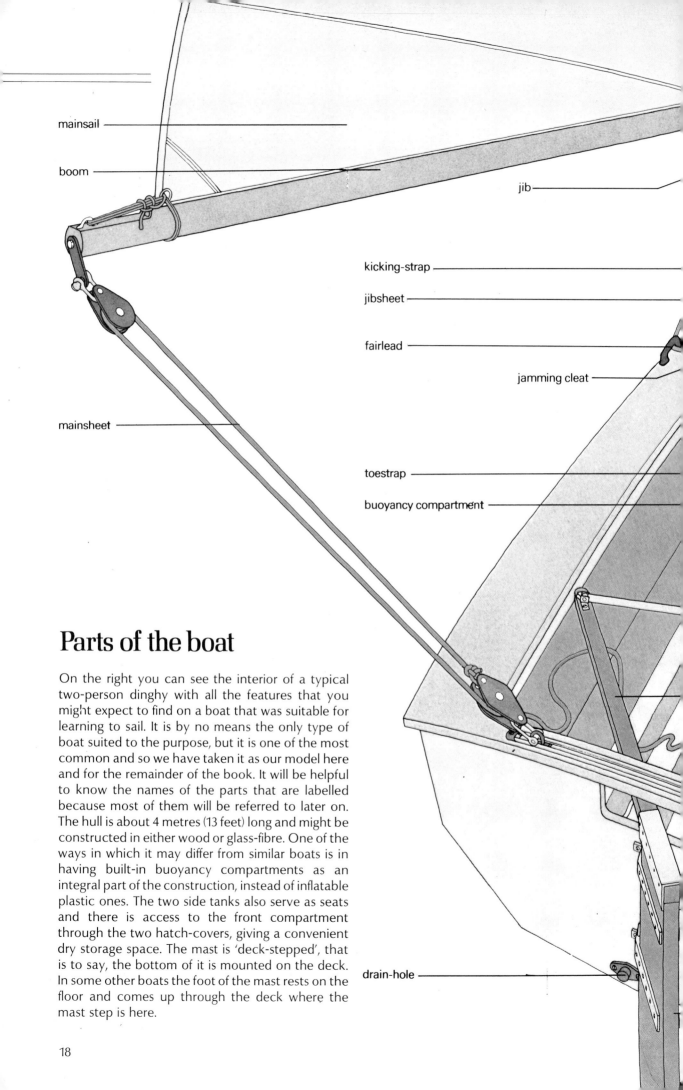

mainsail

boom

jib

kicking-strap

jibsheet

fairlead

jamming cleat

mainsheet

toestrap

buoyancy compartment

Parts of the boat

On the right you can see the interior of a typical two-person dinghy with all the features that you might expect to find on a boat that was suitable for learning to sail. It is by no means the only type of boat suited to the purpose, but it is one of the most common and so we have taken it as our model here and for the remainder of the book. It will be helpful to know the names of the parts that are labelled because most of them will be referred to later on. The hull is about 4 metres (13 feet) long and might be constructed in either wood or glass-fibre. One of the ways in which it may differ from similar boats is in having built-in buoyancy compartments as an integral part of the construction, instead of inflatable plastic ones. The two side tanks also serve as seats and there is access to the front compartment through the two hatch-covers, giving a convenient dry storage space. The mast is 'deck-stepped', that is to say, the bottom of it is mounted on the deck. In some other boats the foot of the mast rests on the floor and comes up through the deck where the mast step is here.

drain-hole

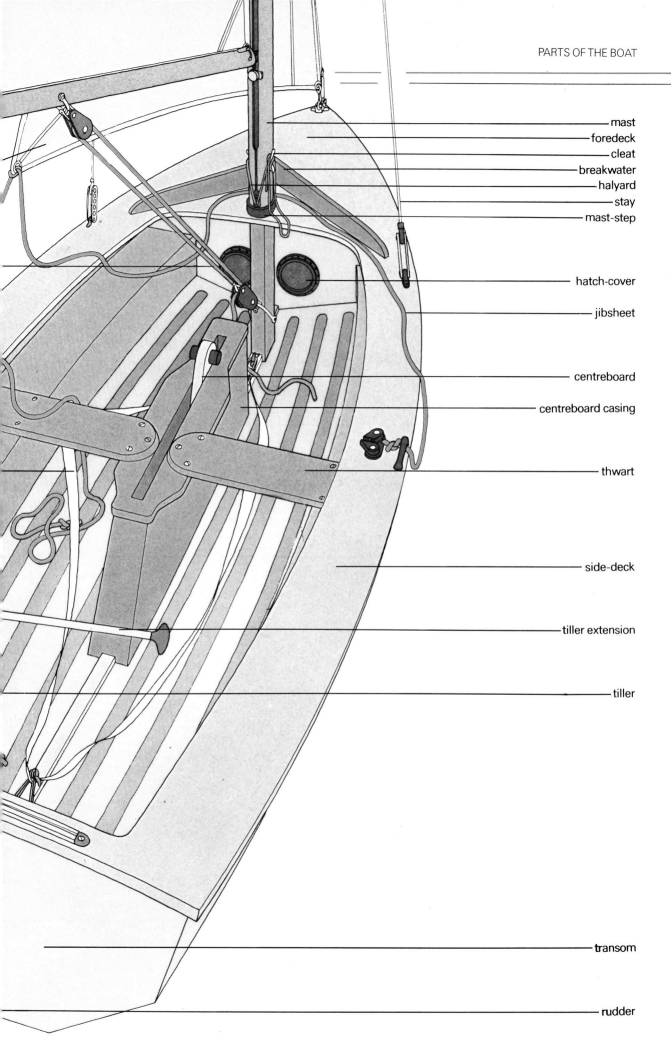

mast
foredeck
cleat
breakwater
halyard
stay
mast-step

hatch-cover

jibsheet

centreboard

centreboard casing

thwart

side-deck

tiller extension

tiller

transom

rudder

Steering systems

A dinghy is steered by means of the rudder which projects down under the back of the boat and deflects the water as it passes. It is controlled by a long handle known as a 'tiller'.

Rudders have to be strong enough to withstand considerable pressure. They are made of wood or, sometimes, of alloy. Some dinghy rudders are made all in one piece. These have to be removed when the boat enters shallow water. Others are pivoted near the top, like the one shown here, so that the blade can be raised clear of the bottom. When sailing normally, the rudder is lowered by pulling a control line which emerges from the top, just underneath the tiller. To hold the rudder down against the pressure of the water, the control line is fastened to a 'cleat' on the underside of the tiller. To raise the rudder the control line is released.

The rudder is hinged onto the back of the boat at two points. Each hinge consists of a 'gudgeon' and a 'pointle' which fits into it. Like the rudder itself, these fittings have to be extremely strong. They are so designed that the rudder can be removed easily by lifting it up and off. It can then be stored inside the boat when not in use.

The tiller is usually made of wood and fits into the top of the rudder. When sailing, it is held in position by a pin. On most modern dinghies there is also a tiller extension, often made of aluminium. This enables the Helmsman to steer while sitting on the side of the boat where he would otherwise be unable to reach the tiller. The extension is generally attached to the tiller by means of a universal joint, which enables it to turn in any direction so that the Helmsman can operate the tiller from any angle.

Some smaller dinghies have a 'dagger-board' instead of a conventional centreboard. This is not pivoted, but is simply raised or lowered vertically. When not in use it can be pulled right out of the casing and stored in the bottom of the boat, like the rudder.

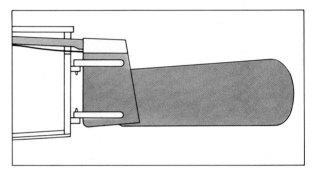

Back of the boat showing how the rudder is mounted on the gudgeons and pintles. The rudder is in the raised position

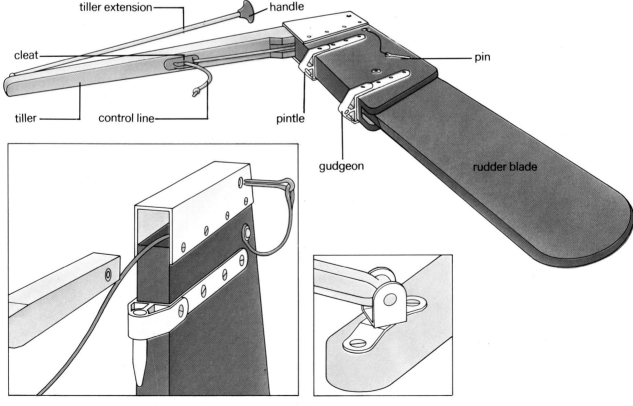

Top of a rudder showing the hole where the end of the tiller is inserted, and the pin which passes through the rudder to hold it in place. The rope is for lowering the blade

Universal joint connecting the tiller extension to the end of the tiller

Centreboards

The centreboard is like a fin which projects down into the water through a slot in the bottom of the boat. Its purpose is to prevent the boat from being blown sideways and it is retractable so that it can be raised up into the boat when not needed.

It is mounted in a casing in the middle of the boat. The sides of the casing have to be higher than the level of the water outside the boat so that water does not get in. The centreboard is pivoted on a bolt which passes through the casing and through a hole in the centreboard itself. It can be removed from the casing for periodic maintenance by removing the bolt.

Centreboards are usually made of wood or alloy. They are roughly rectangular in shape, with a small projection at the top which sticks out of the top of the casing and serves as a handle for raising or lowering it. Since wood weighs about the same as water, a wooden centreboard can easily be raised and lowered by hand. There is usually a piece of rubber screwed onto the top of the centreboard which grips the sides of the casing and prevents it from floating up when it is supposed to be lowered.

In the case of an alloy centreboard, since alloy is rather heavier than water, there is generally a system of pulleys to help raise it. One of the best systems has a control line led to each side of the boat, with a quick-release cleat to hold it, so that the Crew can operate the centreboard from wherever he is sitting. With such a system the control line on the opposite side has to be cleated before it is possible to pull the centreboard up.

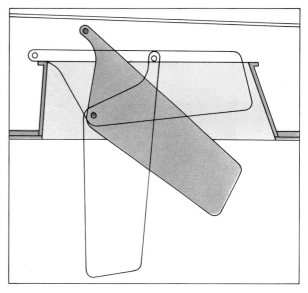

Cut-away view of the centreboard casing showing three different positions of the centreboard. It is pivoted at the front and lowered by means of the handle at the top

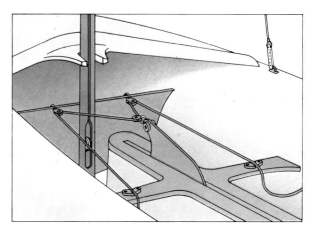

System of ropes and pulley blocks used to hold a centreboard in one position if it is made of alloy. It is arranged so that the centreboard can be raised or lowered from either side

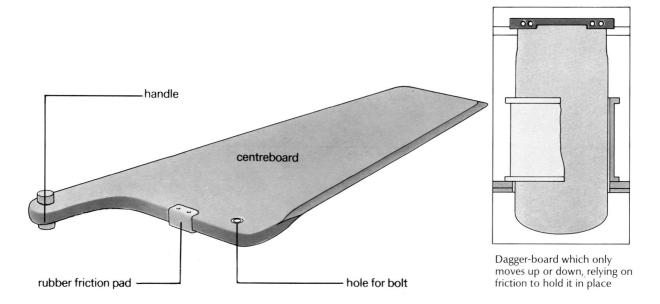

handle

centreboard

rubber friction pad

hole for bolt

Dagger-board which only moves up or down, relying on friction to hold it in place

Mainsheet systems

'Sheets' is the name given to the ropes which control the sails on a sailing boat. In the case of the mainsail, this is a single rope which is attached to the boom and led through a system of pulleys to the Helmsman.

There are two basic types of mainsheet system. With the conventional system one end of the sheet is attached to the back of the boat. From there it passes round a pulley block on the end of the boom and back round a block on the back of the boat, to the Helmsman. The block on the boat is often mounted on a slide which is free to travel from side to side along a track mounted across the back of the boat. Sometimes the position of the slide can be fixed by means of control lines led to either side of the boat.

A more modern system is to have the sheet attached to the middle of the boom, with the track across the middle of the boat. With this system the sheet can be led through a swivelling quick-release cleat mounted in the middle of the boat, so that the Helmsman does not have to hold the sheet at all times. It is also possible to let the sail out some way without releasing the sheet, by releasing the control line which holds the slide in the middle of the track.

Some boats have a combination of both rear and centre systems.

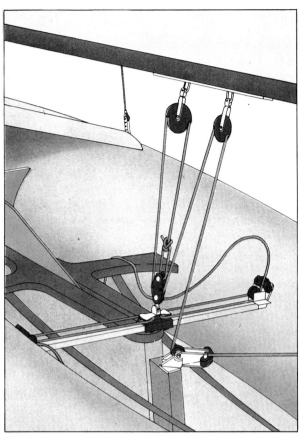

Central mainsheet system where the lower block is attached to a slide which can move along a track across the boat. The position of the slide may be controlled from either side

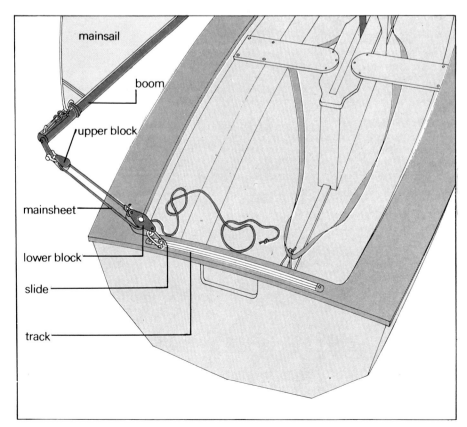

mainsail

boom

upper block

mainsheet

lower block

slide

track

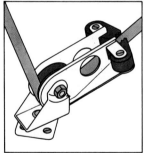

Close-up of the swivelling quick-release cleat of a central mainsheet system

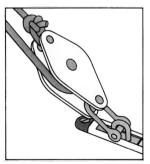

Lower block of a rear mainsheet system

Jibsheet systems

The jib has two sheets, one going to either side of the boat. Only one sheet is ever in use at one time, depending which side the sail is on. The two sheets are usually formed of a single piece of rope which is attached in the middle to the corner of the sail.

Each sheet is led through a 'fairlead', which is a ring fixed on the side of the boat. Beside the fairlead there is a quick-release cleat which keeps the sheet in so that the Crew does not have to hold it the whole time. These quick-release cleats, known as 'jamming cleats', have been mentioned elsewhere and the diagram on the right shows how they are used. You pull the rope downwards over the jaws until they open and it is held securely between them. It will not run out if you let go, but you can pull it in further by pulling at the same angle. To release it, all you have to do is jerk the rope in a bit more, pulling upwards at the same time.

Sometimes, both fairlead and cleat are mounted on a track so that they can be moved a few centimetres backwards or forwards. This is of use if you are 'tuning' the sails for different wind strengths (see Section 8). On some boats the fairlead and cleat are replaced by a 'ratchet block'. Like a jamming cleat this will take the strain on the rope, but only as long as slight tension is kept on it. So the Crew must be sure to hold the jibsheet in his hands at all times.

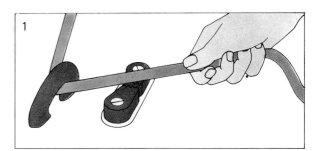

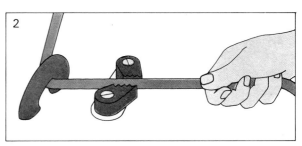

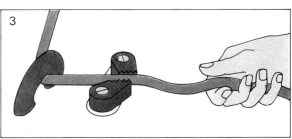

Method of securing a sheet in a jamming cleat. 1. Pull the sheet in over the cleat. 2. Pull it inwards and downwards until it is between the jaws. 3. The sheet is now secure

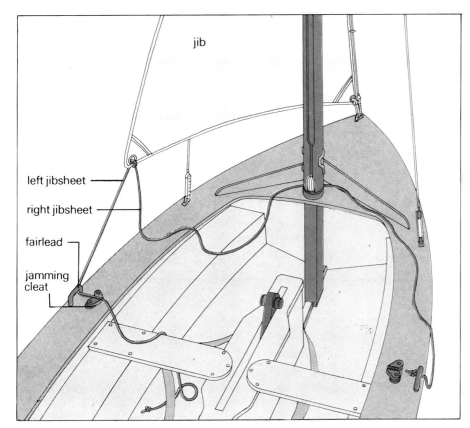

jib

left jibsheet

right jibsheet

fairlead

jamming cleat

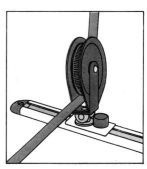

'Ratchet block'. An alternative way of holding a sheet if slight tension is kept on it

Moveable jibsheet fairlead and jamming cleat

23

Mast, boom and rigging

A few years ago the mast and boom of a sailing dinghy were always made of wood, but today they are usually made of aluminium alloy which is strong, light and virtually non-corrosive. They both have a groove on one side to take the bolt-rope around the edge of the mainsail. The end of the boom is hinged onto the mast a few centimetres above deck level by means of a special joint called a 'gooseneck'. This is a spigot mounted on the mast which fits into a square socket in the end of the boom and allows the boom to swing out on either side. When the mainsail is hoisted the boom is held onto the gooseneck by the tension of the sail. When it is lowered the boom comes off the mast and can be laid inside the boat.

The mast is held upright by three wires, one attached to the front of the boat (the 'forestay') and one attached to either side (the 'side-stays' or 'shrouds'). They are attached to the mast at a point about two-thirds of the way up. At the bottom there are adjustable terminals which can be of two basic types, both shown on the right. The 'bottlescrew' type is adjusted by screwing up the two threaded ends. When the stay is tight enough it is wise to wrap copper wire or waterproof tape around it to stop it coming unscrewed. The other type consists of two plates with a series of holes in them. You choose the pair of holes for the tension you want and put a pin through both plates with the loop at the bottom of the stay between them. To keep the pin in place you put a split ring, which is like a kind of key ring, through the hole in the end.

The purpose of the 'kicking-strap', or 'vang' as it is sometimes called, is to keep the boom horizontal

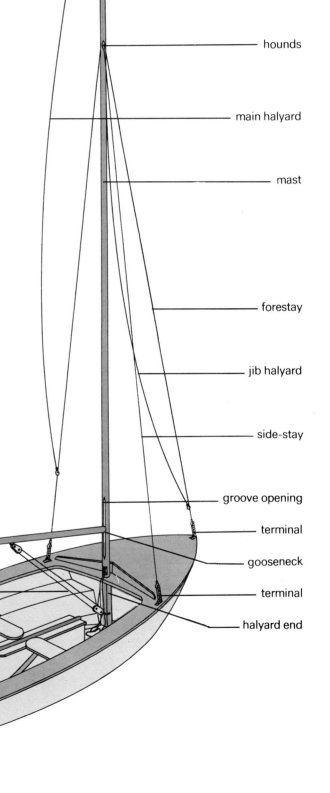

hounds

main halyard

mast

forestay

jib halyard

side-stay

boom

groove opening

terminal

gooseneck

kicking-strap

terminal

halyard end

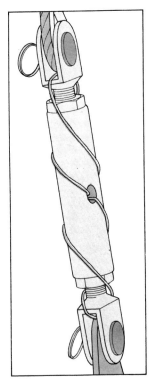

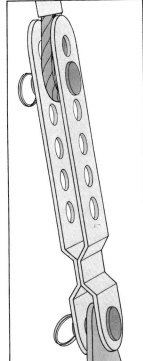

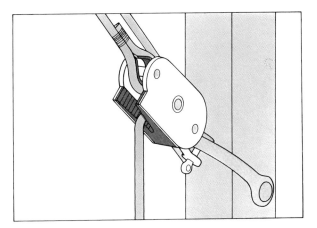

Lower block of a basic kicking-strap system. When tight the end of the rope is locked in the V-shaped slot

Bottlescrew wired to stop it working loose

Stay adjustment with plates and a moveable pin

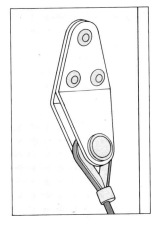

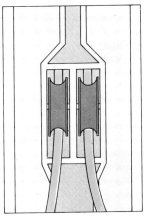

Method of attaching stays to the mast at the 'hounds'

Exit point of the halyards at the base of the mast

Revolving drum type of kicking-strap adjustment. The end of the control line is held in a conveniently placed cleat

and stop the end of it rising up into the air under the pressure of the mainsail. It takes a lot of strain and a considerable amount of force is required to apply the necessary tension in strong winds. A simple solution is to have a two-part purchase with one block on the boom and another mounted low down under the mast. When the rope has been tightened it is made secure by tugging the free end down into a V-shaped slot in one of the blocks. A more elaborate arrangement consists of a revolving drum with a control line wrapped around it. The kicking-strap itself is a length of wire, the end of which is wrapped around the spindle of the drum, in the opposite direction to the control line. To tighten it you just have to pull the control line which takes in the wire at a ratio of about 4-to-1.

The sails are hoisted by means of 'halyards' which are either rope or else wire and rope, joined together inside the mast, so that the part you haul on is rope, while the part that takes the strain when the sail is hoisted is wire. The main halyard enters the mast near the top and the jib halyard just below the forestay. Both run down inside the mast and emerge at the bottom. Once the sail has been hoisted the end of the halyard is secured to a cleat, usually mounted on one side of the mast, in the same way as the flag halyard (see page 35). The ends of the halyards should then be coiled up out of the way.

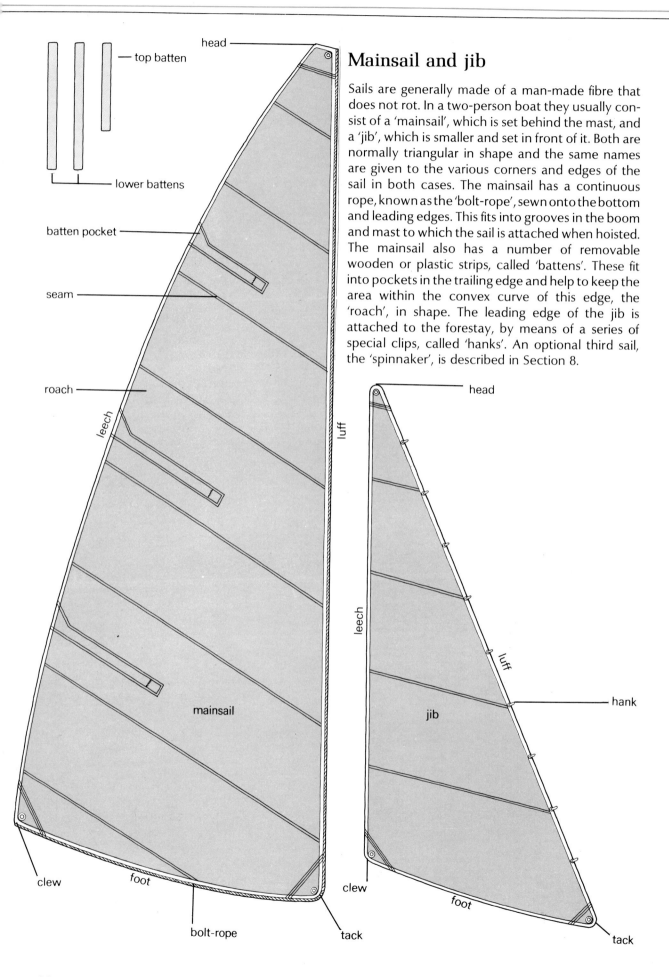

top batten

lower battens

batten pocket

seam

roach

leech

luff

mainsail

clew

foot

bolt-rope

tack

head

Mainsail and jib

Sails are generally made of a man-made fibre that does not rot. In a two-person boat they usually consist of a 'mainsail', which is set behind the mast, and a 'jib', which is smaller and set in front of it. Both are normally triangular in shape and the same names are given to the various corners and edges of the sail in both cases. The mainsail has a continuous rope, known as the 'bolt-rope', sewn onto the bottom and leading edges. This fits into grooves in the boom and mast to which the sail is attached when hoisted. The mainsail also has a number of removable wooden or plastic strips, called 'battens'. These fit into pockets in the trailing edge and help to keep the area within the convex curve of this edge, the 'roach', in shape. The leading edge of the jib is attached to the forestay, by means of a series of special clips, called 'hanks'. An optional third sail, the 'spinnaker', is described in Section 8.

head

leech

luff

jib

hank

clew

foot

tack

Accessories

In addition to the boat itself, there are certain other pieces of equipment that you will need before you start sailing. Unless your boat is light enough to be carried, you will need a **launching trolley** to take it down to the water. These are usually adjustable to accommodate different shapes of boat. A small **anchor** is an extremely valuable safety precaution. The folding type is best. Ideally, there should be at least five times as much anchor rope as the depth of water in which you expect to be sailing. (An anchor will not dig into the bottom if there is not enough rope.) One or more **paddles** is also essential, in case you are becalmed or suffer gear failure which prevents you from sailing. A **sponge** is useful for mopping up small amounts of water in the boat, and a scoop-type **bailer** is good for larger amounts. A plastic **bucket** is really the only reliable way of removing large quantities of water after a capsize. All the last four items should be securely tied into

the boat to prevent them floating away if you do capsize. There should also be a **lifejacket** for each person on board and they should be worn at all times. A stainless steel **sailing knife**, preferably incorporating a 'marlin spike', is handy for all sorts of jobs around the boat. Lastly, a triangular **pennant** which is flown at the top of the mast will help you to gauge the wind direction. The square type is just as effective, but it is really intended for racing.

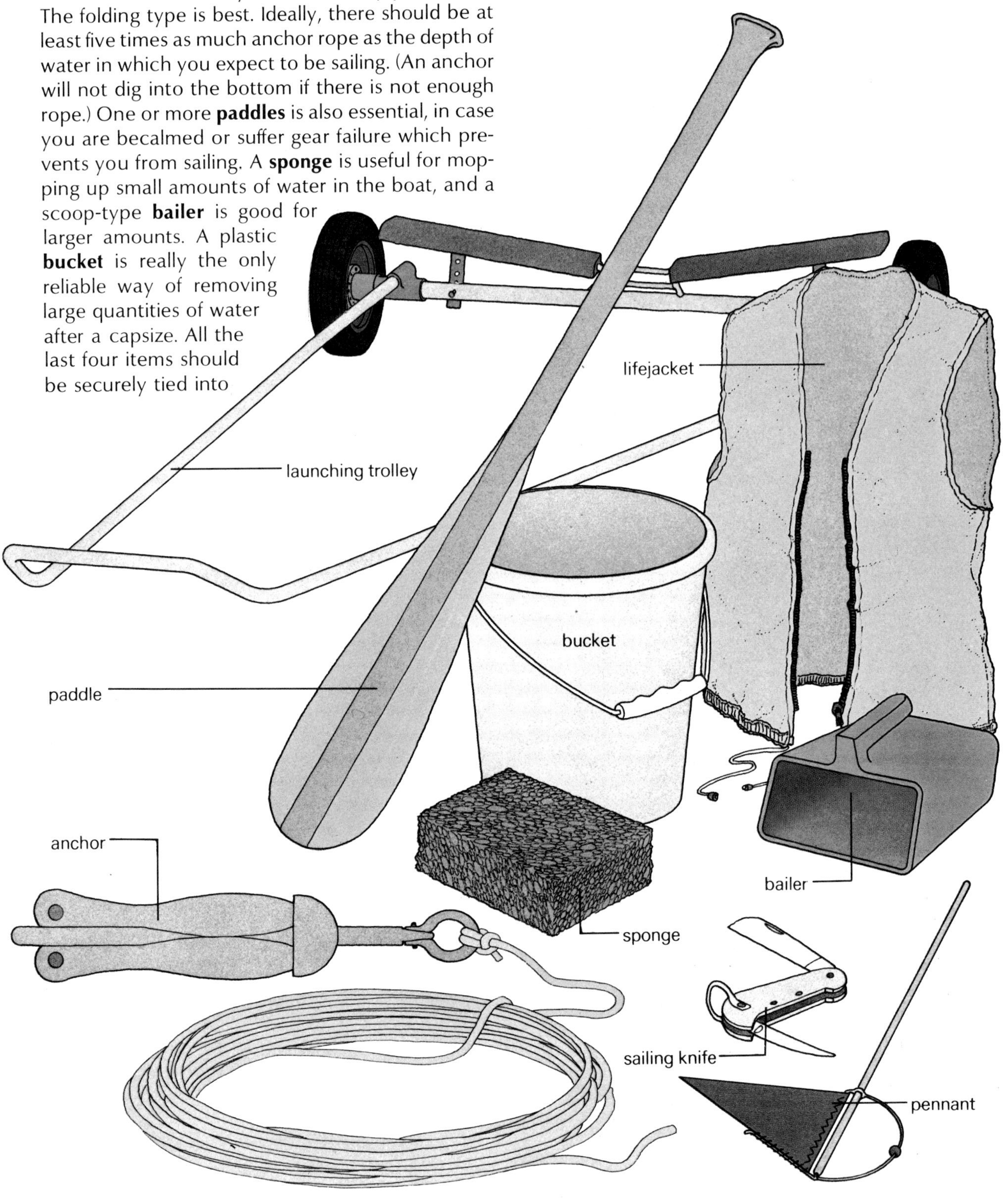

lifejacket

launching trolley

bucket

paddle

anchor

bailer

sponge

sailing knife

pennant

How a boat sails

We have now looked at all the principal working parts of a sailing dinghy and are in a position to see how they combine to make the boat move through the water. Obviously, the sails play the most important part in this process, but the centreboard is also vital.

It is by no means essential to understand exactly how a boat sails in order to be able to sail it. Many perfectly competent sailors have only a shadowy grasp of this subject. Sailing is much more like an art than a science and a good sailor sails by instinct rather than scientific know-how. Nevertheless, though knowing the theory of sailing will not automatically make you a better sailor, it will certainly help you to get the best performance from your boat and may well help you to get extra enjoyment from sailing it.

The first essential is to think of the wind as a moving body of air which flows and eddies rather like the current of a river. When it encounters an obstruction it looks for the easiest way around it, as a river does when it meets a fixed object in its path. In the diagrams on the right the flow of air is represented by the light blue arrows and the diagrams show what happens when it meets an obstruction in the form of the sails of a boat, represented by the thick black lines. Obviously, the diagrams give a rather simplified picture of what goes on, but they show the basic principles of how a boat sails.

The boats on the right are sailing at three different angles to the wind. It is easy enough to understand how a boat sails with the wind *behind* it, as the left-hand one is doing. On the other hand, it is quite difficult to understand how a boat makes progress *against* the wind, as the right-hand one is doing, since its motive power is coming from the opposite, or nearly the opposite, direction. The best way to understand this is to try and visualize what is happening in the middle diagram, where the boat is moving at right-angles to the wind. This should not be too hard if you bear in mind that the boat's centreboard effectively prevents it from moving sideways. Then, by applying the same principles to the boat which is sailing against the wind, it should be possible to see how that, too, is able to make progress in a forward direction.

You will notice that in each of the diagrams the sails are at a different angle to the boat. This is accomplished by hauling in or letting out the sheets which, as we have seen, control the angle of the sails. Having the sails at the correct angle to the wind is the key to making a boat sail, as you will see in Section 4.

Sailing with the wind behind This is easy to understand. Indeed, the boat would get blown along even without any sails, the only difference being that with sails it gets blown along a good deal faster. It also makes no difference whether the centreboard is lowered, since there is no tendency for the boat to get pushed sideways because the wind and boat are moving in the same direction. The sails have been spread out at right-angles to the wind on opposite sides of the boat in order to block as much of the wind as possible. When it meets them it tries to push them out of the way and propels the boat forwards in the process. Because the boat is moving slower than the wind, the air swirls around, looking for a way past the sails. If the boat was moving at the same speed as the wind this would not happen, but the boat could not move faster than the wind because the sails would then act as air-brakes, slowing it down. This is what happens if you sail into a patch of no wind.

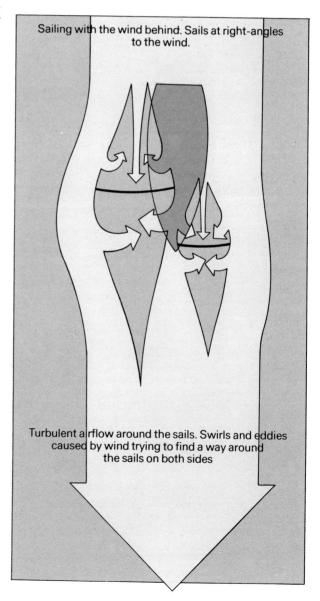

Sailing with the wind behind. Sails at right-angles to the wind.

Turbulent airflow around the sails. Swirls and eddies caused by wind trying to find a way around the sails on both sides

Sailing at right-angles to the wind Here the picture looks completely different. The sails have been hauled in by about 45 degrees and on this course the centreboard would have to be lowered, at least partly, because the wind is trying to push the boat sideways. But the main difference between this and the last diagram is that now the wind is meeting the sails at an angle and flowing parallel to them, instead of meeting them head-on and escaping round both sides. The sails are *diverting* the airflow, instead of *blocking* it, and there is a smooth current of air past the sails in place of the swirls and eddies of the previous diagram. As the air flows along the sails it presses against them and this is what pushes the boat forwards. On this course there is nothing stopping a boat going faster than the wind, which is exactly what some boats, such as catamarans, can do, and all modern boats go faster at right-angles to the wind than they do with it directly behind.

Sailing against the wind The picture has changed again, but not as much as last time. The sails have been hauled in a bit further, so that they are still diverting the wind backwards, but there is an unbroken flow of air past them, as in the previous diagram. In fact, the same principles apply as before, and the boat is being propelled forwards in exactly the same way. If this is difficult to visualize, try to imagine the boat gradually altering course from the last diagram to this one, and see if anything has really changed. The wind is still trying to push the boat sideways and so the centreboard is still lowered. But it is pressing against the sails in more or less the same direction. The sails are at less of an angle to the boat, so there is more sideways force and more centreboard is needed. But there is still forwards pressure and the boat will move forwards, though more slowly than it did at right-angles to the wind, as a result. To look at the situation more closely, see the next page.

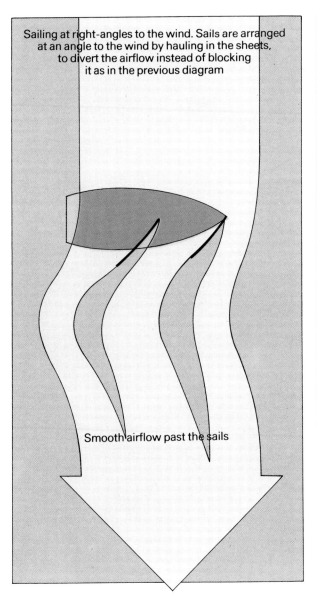

Sailing at right-angles to the wind. Sails are arranged at an angle to the wind by hauling in the sheets, to divert the airflow instead of blocking it as in the previous diagram

Smooth airflow past the sails

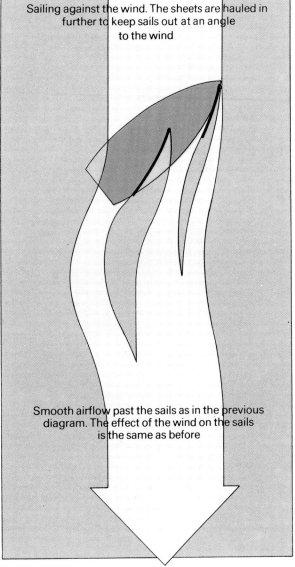

Sailing against the wind. The sheets are hauled in further to keep sails out at an angle to the wind

Smooth airflow past the sails as in the previous diagram. The effect of the wind on the sails is the same as before

Sailing against the wind

We have just seen that the sails of a boat are able to convert the force of the wind into motion in almost the opposite direction to the wind itself. At first sight this may look almost like magic, rather like being able to defy the law of gravity. To understand it better we will look at the phenomenon in more detail.

The diagram on the right shows the same situation as the diagram on the last page, except that, instead of showing two sails, it shows only one. This is because the wind acts on both sails in the same way and so one explanation will do for both. The orange arrow represents the force of the wind against the sail. As the air flows along the sail it presses against it, as a river does around the outside of a bend. This creates a force at right-angles to the surface of the sail.

The direction of this force, relative to the boat, is sideways and slightly forwards, and the orange arrow can be broken down into two different forces at right-angles to one another. The sideways component is shown by the red arrow and the much smaller forwards component by the yellow one. As we have seen, the sideways force is effectively blocked by the centreboard. If the centreboard were raised the boat would be blown sideways and would hardly move forwards at all. In practice, even with the centreboard lowered, a boat will make a little sideways progress, which is known as 'leeway'. This means that the boat does not move in exactly the direction in which it is pointing but, rather, diagonally. In a properly designed boat, however, the amount of leeway is so small as to be negligible. Since it is prevented from moving the boat sideways, the red arrow expends its energy in trying to blow the boat over on its side. This is why boats lean over with the wind. To counteract it the crew of a sailing dinghy move their weight over to the opposite side of the boat, to act as a counterbalance to the force of the wind.

This leaves us with only the yellow arrow, which is pointing in the same direction as the boat. This is the force that makes the boat move forwards against the wind.

Perhaps the most difficult part of this explanation is the reason why the wind does not push the sail backwards, and the boat with it. This is why the fact that the wind is flowing parallel to the sail is of such importance. Every part of the boat that the wind meets head-on, such as the hull, is being pushed backwards, and the sails, in fact, have to overcome this force as well as driving the boat in

Opposite: Sailing against the wind. The force of the wind against the sails is lifting the further hull of this "Tornado" catamaran completely clear of the water

the opposite direction. However, the sails themselves are delicately angled so that they divert the wind without getting pushed backwards.

A modern sailing dinghy is a highly efficient machine for sailing against the wind. The old square-riggers could make very little progress against it, if any, and had to rely on getting a favourable wind to take them where they wanted. However, not even a sailing dinghy can sail directly into the eye of the wind. The nearest you can get to that is an angle of about 45 degrees to the wind direction. In order for the boat to make progress against the wind, the sails have to deflect it. And the only way the sails could deflect it, if the boat was pointing straight into the wind, is if they were pushed out on one side or the other, which would have the effect of pushing the boat backwards. A dinghy does make progress directly against the wind, however, by sailing at 45 degrees, first to one side of the wind direction, and then to the other.

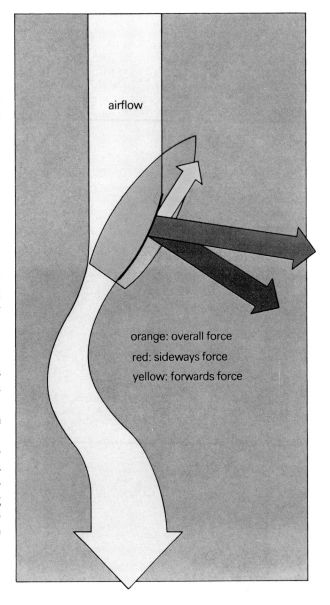

airflow

orange: overall force

red: sideways force

yellow: forwards force

3. Preparing the Boat

When a boat is taken out of the water at the end of a day's sailing the sails are taken off and folded up, and the rudder and tiller are removed and stored in the bottom of the boat. So before you go sailing you will have to fit the sails, replace the rudder and tiller, and launch the boat into the water. If the mast has been taken down since the boat was last sailed, it will have to be put back up again. Normally, there is no need to lower the mast unless you are putting the boat away for a long time (such as over the winter) or the boat is being stored indoors or taken somewhere by road. So you will not have to put the mast up every time you want to go sailing. However, it is a good idea to lower the pennant when you have finished sailing because if it is left at the top of the mast in all weathers the pennant will soon be frayed to bits, and in this case you will have to hoist it before you go sailing again.

It is easiest to fit the mainsail to the boom and the jib to the forestay while the boat is still on dry land. However, it is best not to mount the rudder until the last moment before you actually sail off because it may get in the way while the boat is being pushed around on the trolley and launched. We will deal with mounting the rudder in a later section when we come to Getting Under Way. We will also deal with hoisting the sails in that section, although some people prefer to hoist the jib before the boat is launched. As it is only a small sail it cannot do much harm by blowing around, provided the sheets are free, but it is definitely unwise to hoist the mainsail before the boat is in the water unless the wind is very light indeed, because it may get blown off the trolley.

Unless it is absolutely unavoidable, do not get into the boat at any time while it is on land since you may strain the hull or damage it. It should be possible to reach everything that you need to reach from outside. Another important point: if your boat has drainholes to let water out of the back, ensure that the corks have been put into these before the boat is launched.

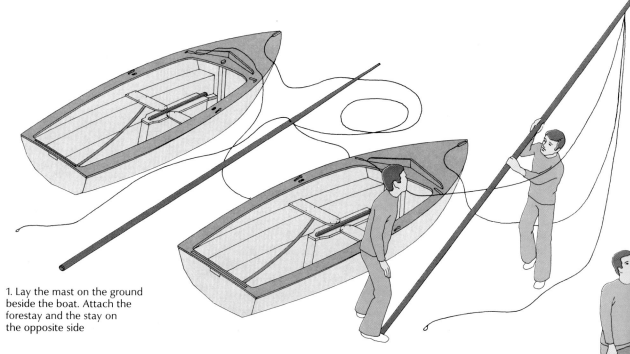

1. Lay the mast on the ground beside the boat. Attach the forestay and the stay on the opposite side

Putting up the mast

The first step when erecting the mast, or 'stepping' it, is to lay it on the ground alongside the boat with the top of the mast nearest the front. Check that the shrouds and the forestay are not tangled and that they will not be twisted when the mast is up. Now attach the forestay to the front of the boat and one of the shrouds, whichever belongs on the side furthest from where the mast is lying, by means of the bottlescrews or shroudplates provided.

The next step is for one person to raise the mast to a vertical position by lifting it near the top and working his way towards the bottom, while the other person keeps the bottom of the mast steady with his foot. He then goes round to the other side of the boat, while the first person holds the mast upright on the ground.

Now, still holding the mast upright, the first person carefully lifts the mast onto the deck. His companion helps him to keep it steady and to manoeuvre the bottom of it into the mast step. Then, while the second person holds the mast upright by pushing it against the pull of the shroud and forestay, the first person attaches the remaining shroud. Finally, you adjust the bottlescrews or shroudplates so that the mast is perfectly vertical and there is no slack to be taken up in the rigging.

2. One person raises the mast, working his way down from the top, while the other steadies its base

3. Second person walks to the other side, while the first holds the mast up

The whole operation is best done when there is not too much wind.

Once the mast is up, you can hoist the pennant. Tie the halyard to the staff at two points, once near the bottom of the pennant and once near the bottom of the staff. A 'clove hitch' is the best knot for the purpose. Now hoist the pennant so that it is free to turn above the top of the mast and fasten the halyard by wrapping it around the cleat on the mast, finishing off by tucking the end under itself, as shown in the drawing (top right).

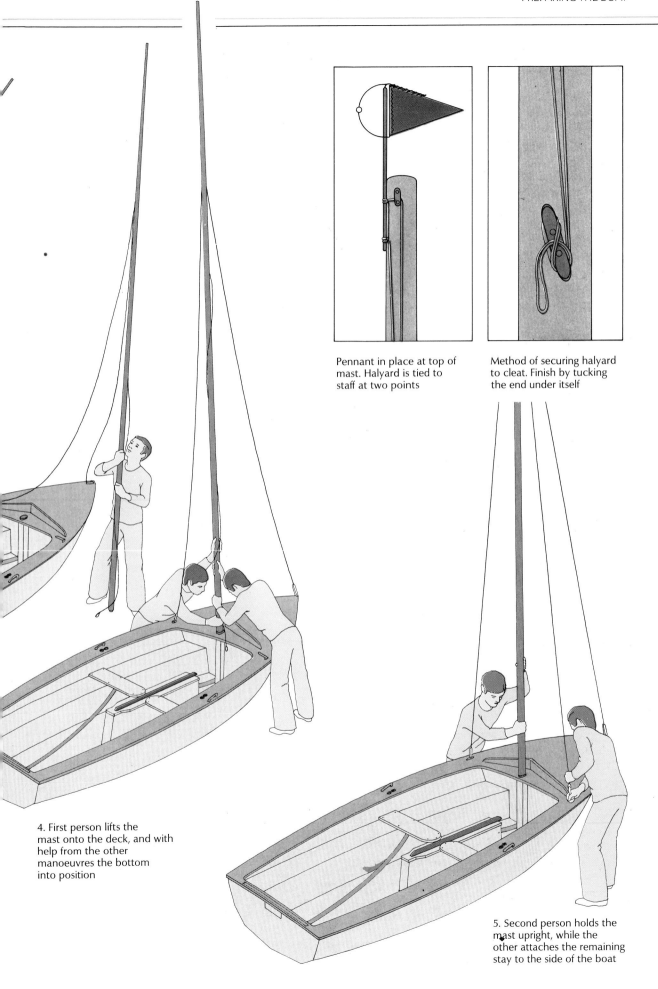

Pennant in place at top of mast. Halyard is tied to staff at two points

Method of securing halyard to cleat. Finish by tucking the end under itself

4. First person lifts the mast onto the deck, and with help from the other manoeuvres the bottom into position

5. Second person holds the mast upright, while the other attaches the remaining stay to the side of the boat

Fitting the mainsail

At the end of a day's sailing the mainsail and jib are taken off the boat and put away. So one of your main jobs before you go sailing will be to fit them back on the boat.

With the mainsail you first have to find the clew of the sail. This is where the bolt-rope (the rope which is sewn all along the foot and luff of the mainsail) begins, and you insert the end of it into the beginning of the groove at the front end of the boom. You then pull the sail along the boom until the foot of the sail is spread the whole way along the boom and the hole in the tack is level with the front end. This job is best done by two people, with one pulling the sail along the boom and the other feeding the bolt-rope into the groove. Now

you put the pin through the sides of the groove and through the hole in the sail, to hold the tack in place. Having done this, you can tension the foot and attach the clew to the rear end of the boom. This is usually done by means of a piece of line attached to the clew, which is threaded a few times backwards and forwards through a ring on the boom and through the sail, adding a few turns around the boom itself.

The next step is to find the head of the sail and attach it by means of a shackle to the loop in the end of the halyard, checking that the halyard is not tangled around the mast before you start. At this stage you can insert the battens into their pockets in the leach of the sail. If the ends are different, the thin end should go in first. Most battens are kept in place by tucking the outer end into a pouch at the end of the pocket, but some pockets are open-ended and the battens have to be tied in place.

Lastly, as a precaution against its being blown around by the wind, you can feed a few centimetres of the head of the sail into the bottom of the groove in the mast. The boom itself need not be fitted to the mast until you are ready to hoist the sail.

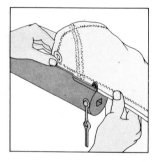

1. Feed the end of the bolt-rope into groove at end of boom, starting at the clew

2. When the bolt-rope has entered the groove as far as the tack, insert the pin

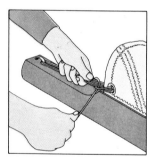

3. Pull the sail tight along the boom, and tie the clew to the end with some line

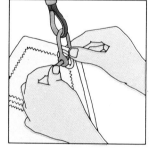

4. Attach the head of the sail to the end of the halyard with a shackle

5. Insert the battens into the pockets in the luff and secure them in place

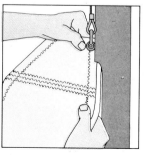

6. Insert the top of the bolt-rope into the bottom of the groove in the mast

When you have finished rigging the boat it should look something like this

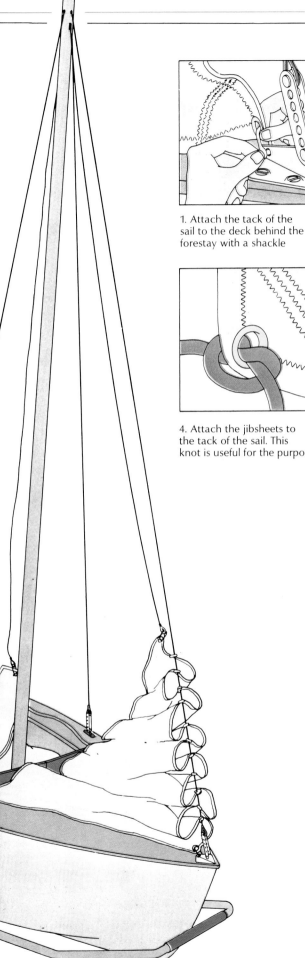

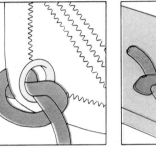

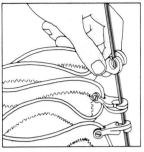

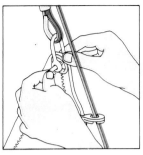

1. Attach the tack of the sail to the deck behind the forestay with a shackle

2. Clip the hanks onto the forestay, starting at the bottom and working up

3. Attach the head of the sail to the end of the halyard with a shackle

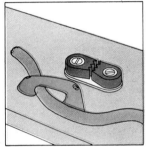

4. Attach the jibsheets to the tack of the sail. This knot is useful for the purpose

5. Thread the end of each sheet through the fairlead, passing it inside the stay

6. Knot the end of the sheet to stop it pulling out. This knot is useful for the purpose

Fitting the jib

The first step is to find the tack of the sail and shackle it onto the ring or loop provided just behind the bottom of the forestay. Starting at the bottom of the sail, clip all the hanks along the luff onto the stay. Check that all of them are on the right way up. Now shackle the head of the sail onto the end of the halyard, taking special care beforehand that the halyard is not twisted around the forestay.

The jibsheets are often not removed from the sail when it is put away. Otherwise, they will have to be re-attached and a good way, if they are made out of a continuous piece of rope, is to tie them onto the hole in the clew of the sail using the knot shown. Thread the end of each sheet through the fairlead on the side of the boat. Generally, the sheet should pass inside the shroud (i.e. between the shroud and the mast). To stop the end of the sheet from running through the fairlead when you are sailing, tie some sort of bulky knot in it. A good type is the figure-of-eight knot, shown above.

After the mainsail and jib have been fitted, the boat should look something like the one on the left. It is now ready for launching. If there is a strong wind, you should be careful that the sails are not caught by it. Keep the mainsail inside the boat and, if necessary, tie the jib down.

Launching the boat

Dinghies are usually put into the water via a slipway or sloping ramp, but if you are launching from a beach the procedure is the same.

Most dinghies are kept on their trolleys while out of the water, but you may need to push the trolley a bit further under the boat before you start to move it down to the water. One person should lift up the front so that the bottom is clear of the trolley, while the other person pushes the trolley further underneath. Ideally, the boat should be more or less evenly balanced over the wheels, with a little more weight at the front. Some people tie a rope around the forestay and the handle of the trolley to stop it slipping off.

Make sure that the rudder and tiller are inside and, most important, that the corks are in the drain-holes at the back. Now the boat can be trundled down to the water. Take care that the bottom does not scrape against the ground as you are pushing it along, because this will damage it.

Push the trolley into the water until the far end is largely submerged. Launching trolleys are designed to take this kind of treatment and it does not harm them. If you are using an ordinary road trailer, on the other hand, you should try to keep it out of the water, because it will damage the bearings.

One person now lifts up the front of the boat and the other pulls out the trolley from under it. While the first person holds onto the boat, the other takes away the trolley. You should leave it somewhere where it will not be in the way of other people launching their boats, and if the tide is out

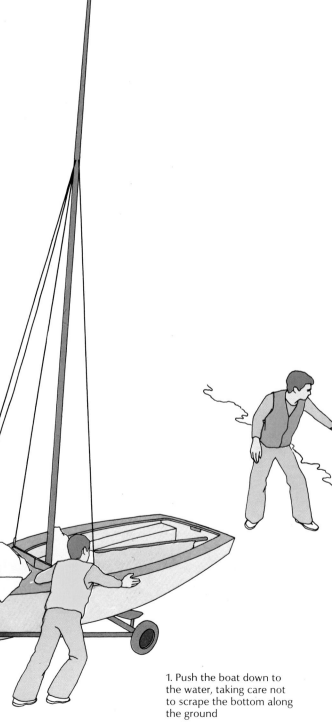

1. Push the boat down to the water, taking care not to scrape the bottom along the ground

38

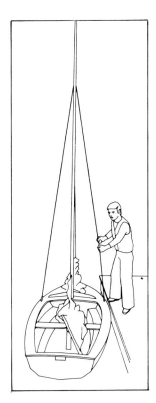

When holding onto a boat which is alongside a quay or landing stage with the wind blowing towards the shore, hold the side-stay, making sure the boat does not damage itself against the shore

3. One person holds the boat, while the other returns the trolley to a safe place

2. Push the trolley into the water until the boat is afloat. Then lift it and pull the trolley out

you should leave it above the high tide mark, or else you may come back and find it under water.

The best way in which to hold onto a boat is by the forestay, so that the front of the boat is pointing into the wind. If the wind is blowing towards the shore you may find that the water is too deep for you to wade out and hold the boat by its front. In that case, you should hold onto the side, as near the front as possible, and keep the boat pointing into the wind from there. Don't let it bump into other boats or you may become unpopular with their owners.

If the boat is floating in deeper water, beside a quay or pontoon, you should still hold onto the forestay if the wind is blowing the boat away from you. But, obviously, if the wind is blowing towards you it will not be possible to keep the boat pointing into the wind. In this case, you will have to hold onto the shroud, making sure that the side of the boat does not bump against the shore.

4. Sailing on One Course

Sailing at a narrow angle to the wind. On this course the sails are pulled in until they are almost parallel to the boat. The Helmsman and Crew of this 'Lark' dinghy have positioned themselves perfectly, so that the boat is dead upright and sailing at maximum speed

Now that the boat is in the water, all that remains to do is hoist the sails, mount the rudder and set off. And so we come to the most important part of the book – handling the boat under sail. This section, on sailing on one course, is in many ways the most important of all, because once you know how to sail the boat correctly on any given course it is a comparatively simple matter to change from one course to another. And when you have mastered that, apart from a few small refinements you have mastered the basic art of sailing.

When you are under sail all that need concern you are four basic 'controls'. One of them, the rudder, we will consider when we come to changing course. The other three are the sheets (main and jib), centreboard and the body weight of the crew members. On some boats there are also certain 'secondary controls', but these can be ignored at this stage since they are not essential to make the boat sail and will be dealt with in a later section. In this section we will take each of these three basic controls in turn. For each one there is a simple rule that will enable you to 'adjust' it correctly for any given course and, in the case of crew weight, for any given strength of wind.

It is important to realise that 'course', in the sense that we are using it here, means the direction in which the boat is travelling *relative to the direction of the wind*. Small changes in wind direction occur perhaps more frequently than non-sailors imagine, and in order to stay on the same course if the wind changed direction the boat would have to change direction too. In practice, obviously, you are more likely to want to sail in a particular direction than stay on one course, or 'point of sailing' as it is sometimes called. What you would have to do then, if the wind changed, would be readjust the controls to take account of your new course relative to the wind. However, for the next few pages we will assume that the wind does not change direction and that 'sailing on one course' is the same as sailing in a straight line.

There is one course that you will not find mentioned in this section – sailing straight into the wind. That is because a boat *cannot* sail into the eye of the wind. But you can make progress in this direction, only it involves changing course at least once. This important manoeuvre, called 'beating', is described in Section 5.

Using the sheets

It is extremely important that both main and jib sheets are correctly adjusted at all times. The correct adjustment is determined by the angle at which the boat is sailing relative to the wind, and every time this angle changes, even slightly, the sheets should be hauled in or eased off a bit to take account of it. The correct sheet adjustment for any given course follows an extremely simple pattern. *The wider the angle between the boat's course and the wind, the more the sheets should be eased off.* Thus, in the drawings on the right, the sheets are hauled right in when the boat is sailing at 45 degrees to the wind direction, they are eased off a little at 90 degrees to the wind, and they are eased right off at 180 degrees or, in other words, when the wind is directly behind the boat. Exactly the same would be true if the boat were sailing from right to left, instead of from left to right, except that the sails would be on the opposite side of the boat. Where the wind is directly behind the boat the sails could in fact be on either side.

When the wind is directly behind the boat the mainsail sometimes cuts off the flow of wind to the jib. In this situation it is better if the Helmsman holds the jib out on the opposite side, a technique known as 'goosewinging'. (See the drawing on the extreme right.)

In a two-person boat the Helmsman manages the mainsheet while the Crew is normally responsible for the jib. The Helmsman has to have one hand on the mainsheet at all times because, except on boats with a centre mainsheet system, there is no other way of stopping it from running out. The Crew is luckier in that there may be a cleat for the jibsheet which can be used to take the strain. However, it is advisable to hold the sheets in the hand even when cleated so that rapid adjustments can be made if necessary. As we have seen, there are two jibsheets, one on either side of the boat, only one of which is ever in use at one time. It is extremely important for the Crew to make sure that the sheet *not* in use is slackened off completely so that it does not interfere with the trim of the sail.

The sails, which the sheets control, are the boat's only source of motive power. Unless they are adjusted at precisely the right angle to the wind at all times, they will not work properly and the boat will go slower as a result. It is not enough simply to judge the wind direction and then move the sheets until you think they are in roughly the right position. A more reliable technique for finding the correct adjustment is needed and this is described over the page that follows.

Sailing at a narrow angle to the wind. Both sheets are hauled tight, so the sails are as far in as possible

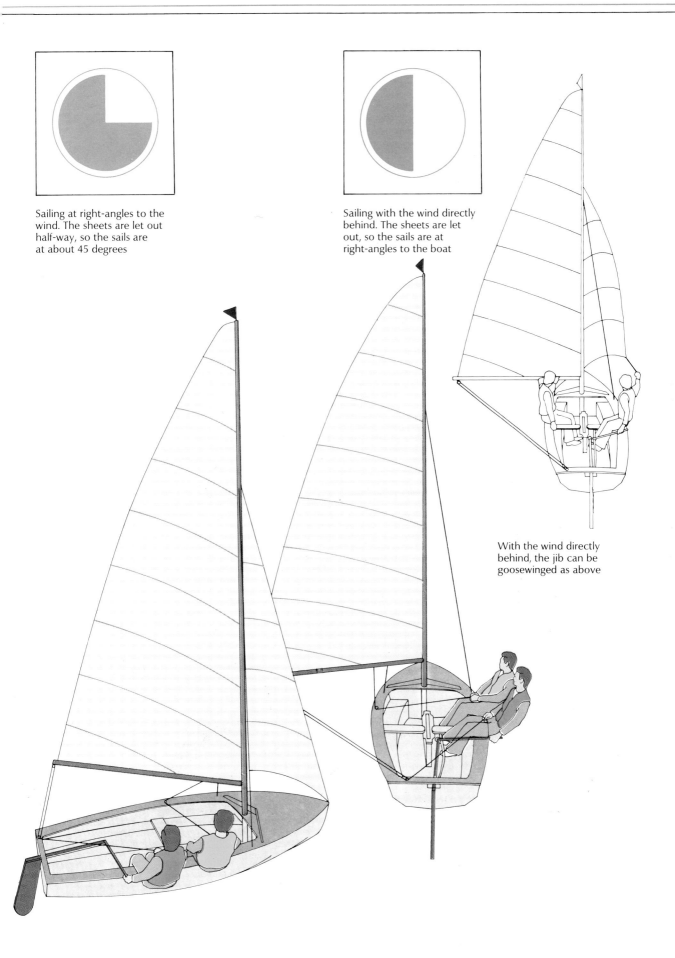

Sailing at right-angles to the
wind. The sheets are let out
half-way, so the sails are
at about 45 degrees

Sailing with the wind directly
behind. The sheets are let
out, so the sails are at
right-angles to the boat

With the wind directly
behind, the jib can be
goosewinged as above

Finding the correct sail angle

The only really accurate way of finding the correct adjustment for the sheets is the one shown below. Start off with the sails flapping; then slowly haul the sheets in. You will notice that as you do so the flapping gradually stops, in the back half of the sail first, and the boat gathers speed. At the moment when the sails have *just* stopped flapping the sail is at precisely the right angle to the wind. If you haul in the sheet any further, although the sail will not start flapping again the boat will start to lose speed.

This procedure works on any course and with either sail, though for simplicity's sake we have only shown the mainsail here. So both Helmsman and Crew should know it. It is much more accurate than trying to estimate the wind direction and work out the correct adjustment from there, although you may want to use that method to give you a rough idea of where the sails should be before you start. You can get some impression of where the wind is coming from by looking at the ripples or waves on the water. Do not rely too much on the pennant; that is only really useful when the wind is behind the

1. Start with the sheet right out. The sail flaps and the boat does not move through the water

2. Haul the sheet in slowly. The back of the sail stops flapping and the boat begins to move forwards

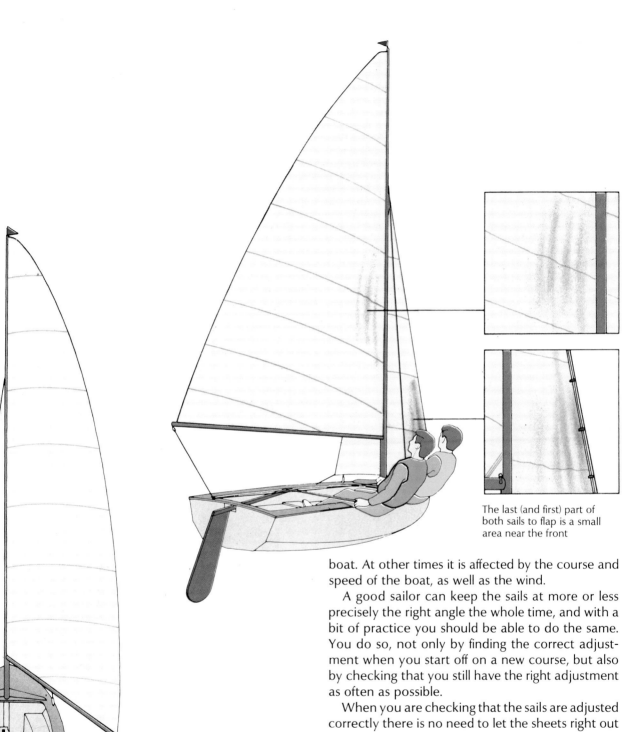

The last (and first) part of both sails to flap is a small area near the front

3. Haul the sheet in further until the front of the sail has just stopped flapping. It is now at the correct angle

boat. At other times it is affected by the course and speed of the boat, as well as the wind.

A good sailor can keep the sails at more or less precisely the right angle the whole time, and with a bit of practice you should be able to do the same. You do so, not only by finding the correct adjustment when you start off on a new course, but also by checking that you still have the right adjustment as often as possible.

When you are checking that the sails are adjusted correctly there is no need to let the sheets right out so that the sails start to flap wildly and the boat loses speed. When you haul the sheets in, the last part of both sails to stop flapping is a small area near the luff or leading edge, about a third of the way up, as shown above. Helmsman and Crew should watch this part of their respective sails as much as possible. To check that your sheet is not hauled in too tight, try letting it out at regular intervals until it starts to flutter at this point. Then haul in until the fluttering stops. Of course, if the luff of the sail starts to flutter of its own accord, you should also haul in the sheet.

Using the centreboard

As with the sheets, the correct position for the centreboard is dictated by the angle at which the boat is sailing relative to the wind. *The narrower the angle between the boat's course and the wind, the more the centreboard should be lowered.* As you can see from the drawings on the right, this means that it should be lowered to its fullest extent when you are sailing at 45 degrees to the wind, about half-way down when sailing at 90 degrees, and raised completely at 180 degrees. Naturally, it will have to be raised if you are sailing in such shallow water that it is scraping the bottom. But the boat may become difficult to steer as a result, and so it is preferable to stay in deeper water except when you are sailing at a wide angle to the wind and the centreboard is raised anyway.

It is sometimes advisable to have the centreboard lowered slightly even when sailing at 180 degrees to the wind (as in the drawing on the extreme right). This makes steering easier and in stronger winds enhances stability. However, you should resist the temptation to lower the centreboard too much in an attempt to stop the boat rolling in strong winds, because this makes steering very difficult indeed and the boat may be impossible to control. The real purpose of the centreboard is to stop the boat being blown sideways, not to keep it upright.

The centreboard is usually operated by the Crew since he can generally reach it more easily than the Helmsman. The Helmsman anyway normally has enough to do in steering the boat and managing the mainsheet. However, if circumstances permit and the Crew is otherwise engaged, there is no reason why the Helmsman should not operate the centreboard on occasions.

The centreboard is a much less critical adjustment than the sheets and does not need to be moved as often. There is generally no need to readjust it unless there is a fairly substantial change in the angle between the boat's course and the wind direction, and minor variations in course and wind direction can be ignored. In practice the three different positions shown on the right are probably all you need. When the wind is light it is perfectly possible to sail with the centreboard right down on any course with only a small loss of speed. As the wind increases, however, it will become progressively more difficult to steer the boat when sailing at a wide angle to the wind and, as we have noted, it is potentially dangerous in strong winds. On the other hand, whatever the strength of wind, if you attempt to sail without any centreboard at all you will find yourself being blown severely sideways unless the wind is directly behind the boat.

Sailing at a narrow angle to the wind. The centreboard is lowered fully

Sailing at right-angles to the wind. The centreboard is raised half-way

Sailing with the wind directly behind. The centreboard is raised completely

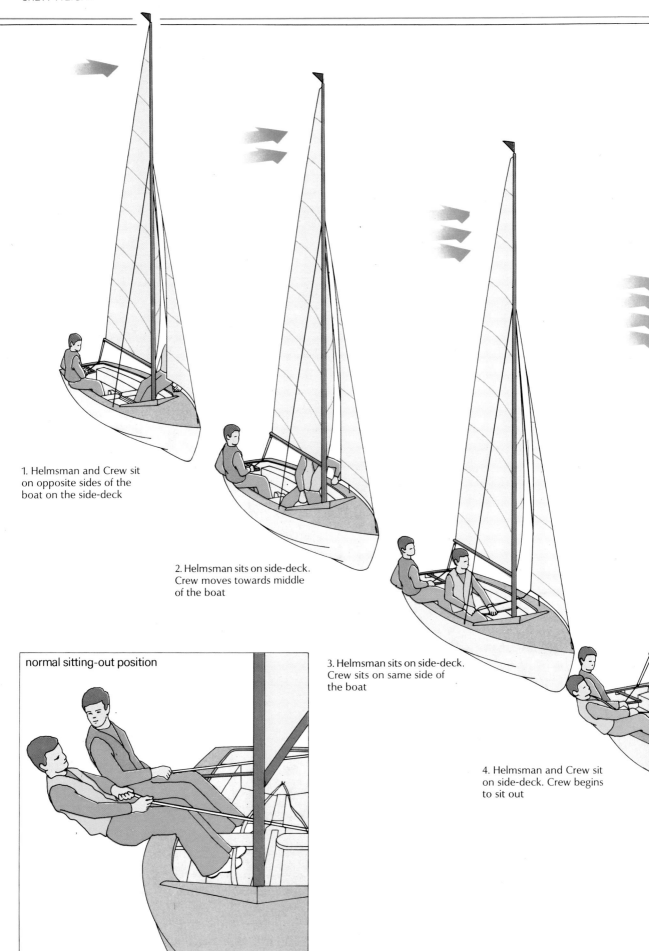

1. Helmsman and Crew sit on opposite sides of the boat on the side-deck

2. Helmsman sits on side-deck. Crew moves towards middle of the boat

3. Helmsman sits on side-deck. Crew sits on same side of the boat

4. Helmsman and Crew sit on side-deck. Crew begins to sit out

normal sitting-out position

Using crew weight

As well as managing the sheets and centreboard, the crew of a sailing dinghy must use their own weight to counterbalance the force of the wind against the sails and prevent the boat from capsizing. The golden rule is: *keep the boat as nearly upright as possible at all times*. This is true on any course and in any wind. Dinghies are designed to be sailed upright and one which is not, though it may look spectacular, is not being sailed well or fast. The only exception to this rule is in very *light* winds, when the boat will sail faster if it is allowed to lean over slightly.

Keeping the boat on even keel is primarily the job of the crew. The Helmsman always needs to be in a position where he has a good view of the sails and activity in the front of the boat, so he normally sits on the side opposite the sails—the 'windward' side. Consequently, the Crew must be prepared to sit on either side, or in the middle, as the occasion demands. Often it will be necessary for one or both crew members to move their weight actually outside the boat, or 'sit out'. It does not matter who is first to sit out, but if the wind is variable in strength (meaning that more weight is required at one moment and less the next) it is better that Crew moves in and out of the boat, while the Helmsman only moves when the Crew's weight alone is not enough. However, Helmsman *and* Crew should be prepared to move quickly when there is a sudden gust or lull in the wind.

If the combined weight of Helmsman and Crew when sitting out is still not enough to keep the boat upright, the Helmsman must release the mainsheet and the pressure of the wind against it is decreased. Don't let go completely, however, or you will both find yourselves in the water. Under exceptional conditions it may be necessary for the Crew to release the jibsheet as well.

Sitting out may look precarious but in fact should be quite comfortable. The correct position is with the instep tucked under the toestraps, and the back of the calves pressing against the inner edge of the side-deck and the back of the thighs against the outer edge. This is shown in the drawing on the far left. Toestraps are generally adjustable and if you are not comfortable try making them longer or shorter.

Although there is no strict relationship between the course you are sailing and the place where you should sit, a boat's *tendency* to lean over, or 'heel', is always greater, the narrower the angle is between its course and the wind. So when you alter course to sail at a narrower angle to the wind you must be ready to move your weight into a position to balance the increased pressure of wind against the sails, and *vice versa*.

5. Helmsman and Crew both sit out. If the boat still tries to heel, the Helmsman lets the mainsheet out slightly

Sitting nearer the back or front

In addition to keeping the boat on an even keel by moving their weight to one side or the other, Helmsman and Crew can make a difference to the performance of a dinghy by moving nearer to the front or the back. This is a much less important consideration than which side you are sitting on, but it is worth watching if you want the boat to sail as fast as possible.

When viewed from in front or behind, the underside of a typical dinghy is flatter towards the back than it is at the front where the cross-section is more V-shaped. By moving your weight towards the relevant end of the boat you can bring more or less of either section into contact with the water. For instance if you sit nearer to the front of the boat more of the V-shaped part will be submerged

and some of the flatter section near the back will be lifted clear of the water.

As a rule, in light winds you should sit forward and in strong winds nearer the back. Your course also makes a difference; at wider angles to the wind you should move towards the back and at narrow angles further forward. In other words, you sit furthest back when you are sailing at a wide angle to the wind direction in a strong wind. These rules apply to both crew-members, and sitting close together will also help the ends of the boat to lift as you go over waves.

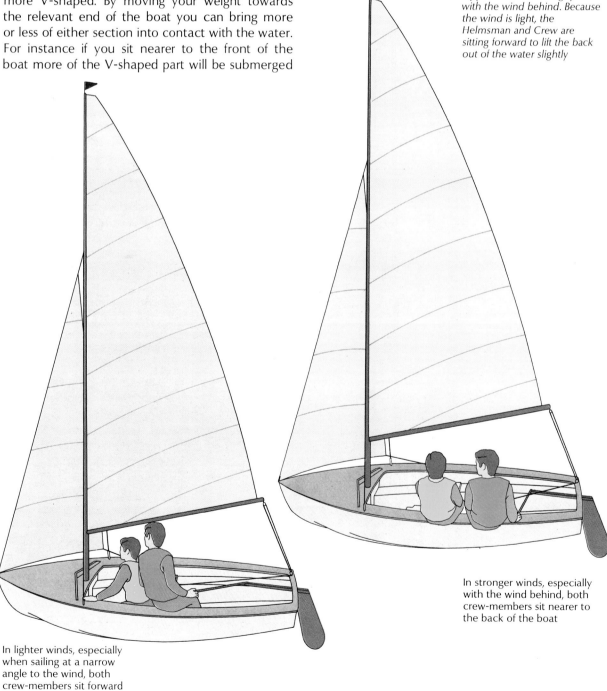

Opposite: A '470' dinghy with the wind behind. Because the wind is light, the Helmsman and Crew are sitting forward to lift the back out of the water slightly

In stronger winds, especially with the wind behind, both crew-members sit nearer to the back of the boat

In lighter winds, especially when sailing at a narrow angle to the wind, both crew-members sit forward

5. Changing from One Course to Another

All you have to do in a motor boat when you want to change course is turn the rudder, but in a sailing boat you have to readjust the controls as well. This is because when you change from one course to another you change the angle at which the boats meets the wind. This means that you have to adjust the sheets and, if the change is a big one, the centreboard for the new course. You must also be ready to counteract any change in the boat's tendency to heel by moving your weight.

There are four basic types of course change. By sailing round in a circle, as in the diagram, you would execute each one in turn. 'Luffing up' and 'bearing away', where the wind (and therefore the sails) stay on the same side of the boat, are a relatively simple matter. However, at two points in the circle the sails cross from one side of the boat to the other; once when the wind is behind the boat, and once when it is in front. These two manoeuvres, known as 'gybing' and 'tacking', may require more practice.

Tacking is needed more often than gybing because it is an integral part of 'beating', a further manoeuvre described at the end of the section, which enables you to make progress straight into the wind.

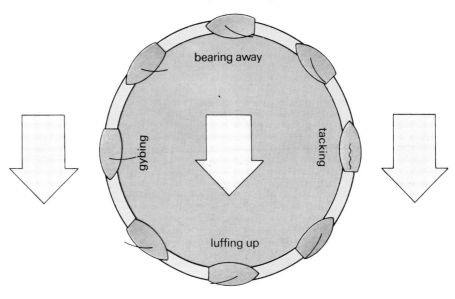

Using the rudder

Before we come to any of the actual manoeuvres we must look at the fourth basic control, the rudder, because this is involved in all of them.

The rudder works by deflecting the water as it passes the back of the boat. The pressure of water against whichever side is turned forwards swings the back of the boat in the opposite direction. Some beginners find it hard to remember which way to turn the rudder to make the boat turn in a particular direction. The rule is: *the boat turns in the opposite direction to the way you move the tiller.* In other words, if you pull the tiller towards you the boat will turn *away* from the side where you are sitting, and *vice versa.*

Turning the rudder has no effect unless there is water flowing past it, and you need a bit of momentum, known as 'steerage way', before you can change course. If it is stationary the boat will not turn. Therefore, you should try to keep the boat moving so that you do not lose control. However if there is very little wind you may be able to make the boat turn by pulling the tiller quickly over to one side.

Apart from this one situation, where the boat has stopped and you need to jerk the rudder to get it turning, the essence of good steering is to avoid violent movements of the tiller. Except in an emergency, do not make sharp changes of course, especially in light winds. If you slam the rudder right over to one side it will bring the boat almost to

2. Move the tiller, and the boat begins to change course

1. Boat is sailing on a straight course with the tiller in its normal position

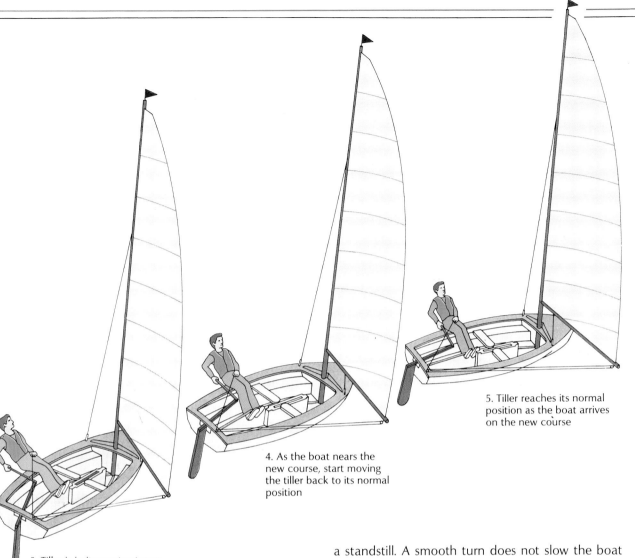

3. Tiller is in its most extreme position when the boat is half-way through the turn

4. As the boat nears the new course, start moving the tiller back to its normal position

5. Tiller reaches its normal position as the boat arrives on the new course

a standstill. A smooth turn does not slow the boat down and also gives you more time to make adjustments to the sheets, centreboard, etc. Move the tiller a little at first, increasing the angle as the boat starts to turn. It should be at the largest angle around the middle of the turn and should arrive back at its normal position at the same moment as the boat reaches its new course.

The 'normal' position for the tiller is not necessarily directly in line with the middle of the boat. To keep the boat on a straight course you may have to hold the tiller slightly nearer to yourself ('weather helm') or slightly further away ('lee helm'). Whether your boat has weather helm, lee helm or neither depends partly on the design of the hull, partly on the sails and partly on the strength of the wind. Many sailors like a boat to have slight weather helm which means that if you let go of the tiller the boat will turn itself until it is pointing into the wind. However, too much of *either* weather helm *or* lee helm will slow the boat down and also make it extremely hard to steer. Excessive weather helm may be caused by not keeping the boat upright enough. It may also be caused, as may excessive lee helm, by the adjustment of the rigging, and a cure for this is given in Section 8.

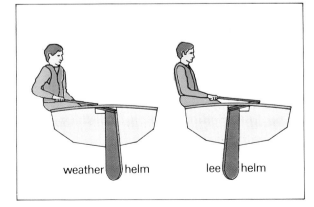

weather helm   lee helm

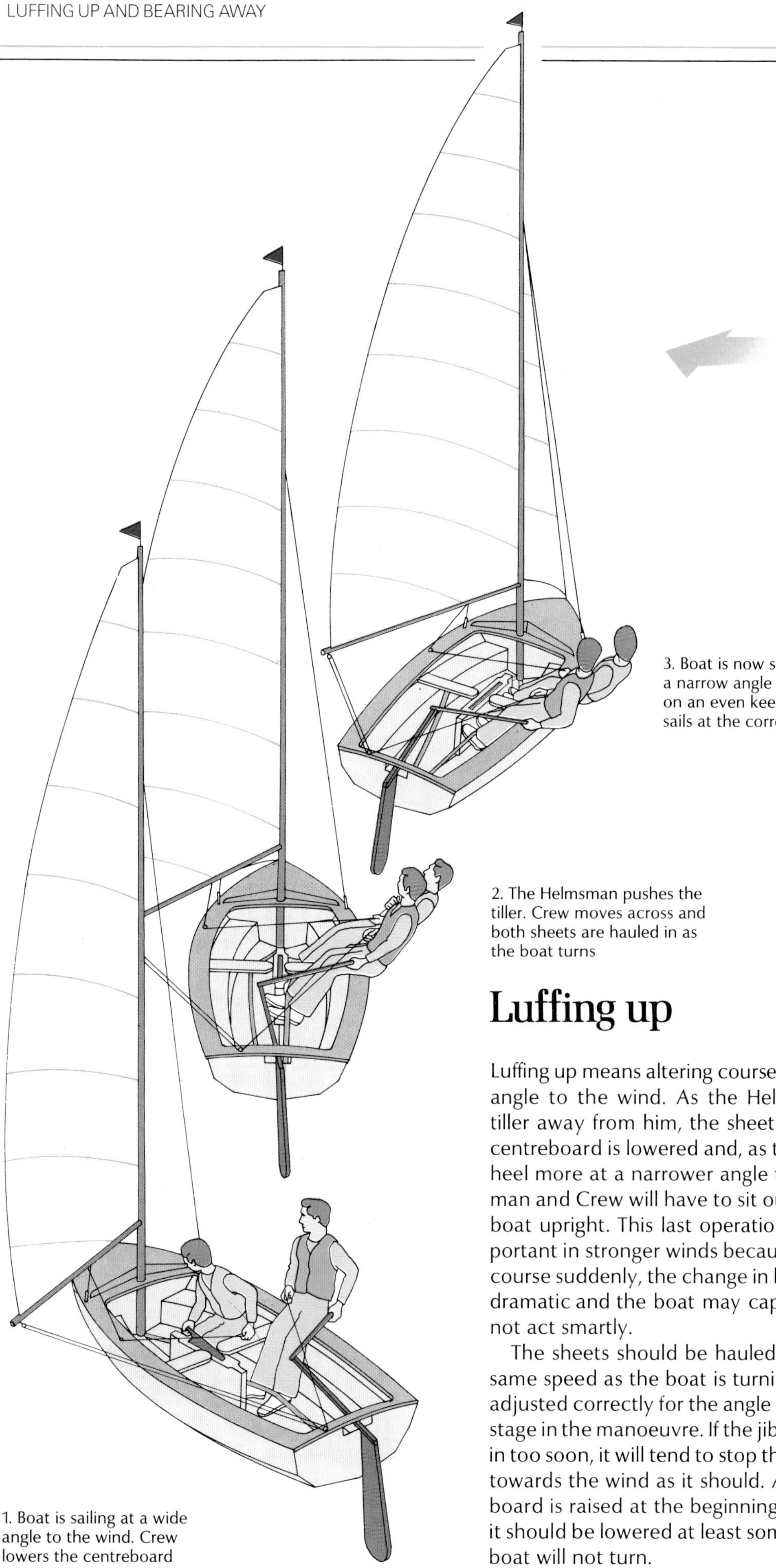

3. Boat is now sailing at
a narrow angle to the wind,
on an even keel, with the
sails at the correct angle

2. The Helmsman pushes the
tiller. Crew moves across and
both sheets are hauled in as
the boat turns

Luffing up

Luffing up means altering course to sail at a narrower
angle to the wind. As the Helmsman pushes the
tiller away from him, the sheets are hauled in, the
centreboard is lowered and, as the boat will tend to
heel more at a narrower angle to the wind, Helmsman and Crew will have to sit out more to keep the
boat upright. This last operation is particularly important in stronger winds because, if the boat alters
course suddenly, the change in heeling can be quite
dramatic and the boat may capsize if the Crew do
not act smartly.

The sheets should be hauled in *gradually*, at the
same speed as the boat is turning, so that they are
adjusted correctly for the angle of the wind at every
stage in the manoeuvre. If the jib especially is hauled
in too soon, it will tend to stop the boat from turning
towards the wind as it should. Again, if the centreboard is raised at the beginning of the manoeuvre,
it should be lowered at least some of the way or the
boat will not turn.

1. Boat is sailing at a wide
angle to the wind. Crew
lowers the centreboard

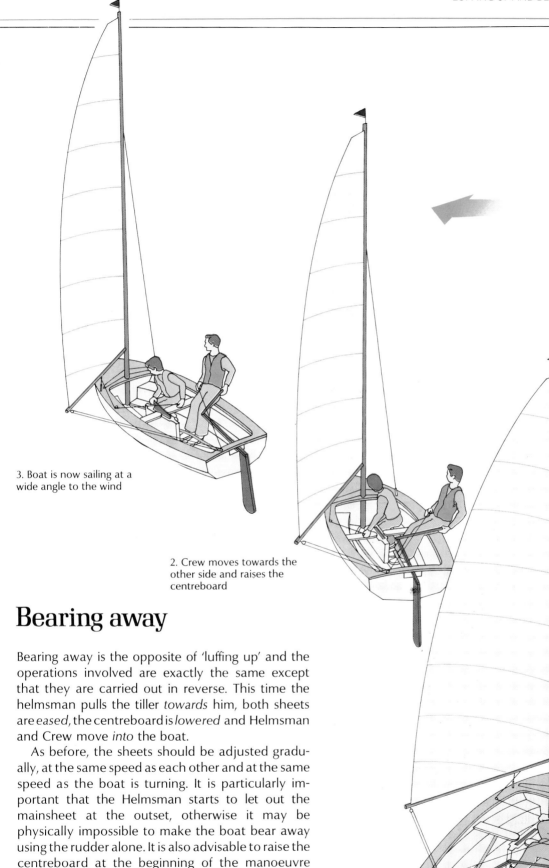

3. Boat is now sailing at a
wide angle to the wind

2. Crew moves towards the
other side and raises the
centreboard

Bearing away

Bearing away is the opposite of 'luffing up' and the
operations involved are exactly the same except
that they are carried out in reverse. This time the
helmsman pulls the tiller *towards* him, both sheets
are *eased*, the centreboard is *lowered* and Helmsman
and Crew move *into* the boat.

As before, the sheets should be adjusted gradually, at the same speed as each other and at the same
speed as the boat is turning. It is particularly important that the Helmsman starts to let out the
mainsheet at the outset, otherwise it may be
physically impossible to make the boat bear away
using the rudder alone. It is also advisable to raise the
centreboard at the beginning of the manoeuvre
because then the boat will bear away much more
readily.

In the case of both bearing away *and* luffing up, it
is best to begin by changing course slowly and wait
until you can do them smoothly before you attempt
a sudden change of course.

1. Helmsman pulls the tiller.
The sheets are let out as
the boat starts to turn

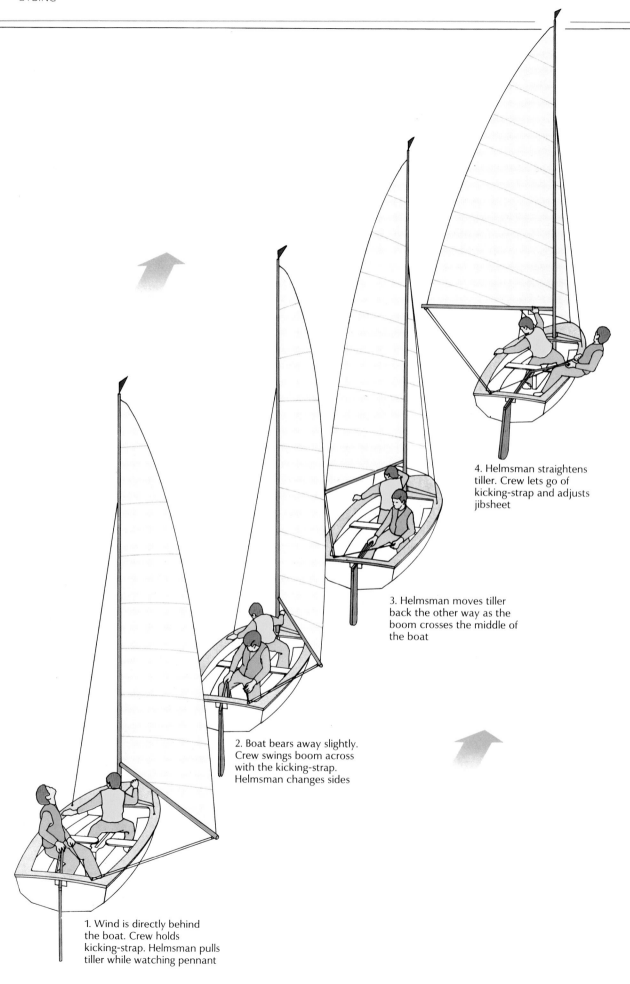

4. Helmsman straightens tiller. Crew lets go of kicking-strap and adjusts jibsheet

3. Helmsman moves tiller back the other way as the boom crosses the middle of the boat

2. Boat bears away slightly. Crew swings boom across with the kicking-strap. Helmsman changes sides

1. Wind is directly behind the boat. Crew holds kicking-strap. Helmsman pulls tiller while watching pennant

Gybing

'Gybing' means bringing the sails from one side of the boat to the other when the wind is directly *behind*. Although this is something that you do when you are changing course, it is best to have the boat sailing in more or less a straight line while the operation is actually carried out.

As we have already seen, when you are sailing with the wind directly behind the boat the sheets are let out until the sails are roughly at right-angles to the boat and the wind. The Helmsman sits facing the mainsail and the Crew sits on the other side to balance the boat. In order to gybe, two things have to happen at the same time: the sails have to be swung across the boat, and the Helmsman and Crew have to change sides. At the end of the gybe the boat will still be sailing on the same course, but everyone and everything will be on the opposite side to where they were.

To know when to gybe the Helmsman must watch the pennant at the top of the mast. When it is pointing straight towards the front of the boat, the wind is directly behind and you are ready to gybe. The Crew gets hold of the kicking-strap just underneath the boom in readiness to swing it across the boat. He releases the jibsheet and leaves the jib to its own devices until the gybe is complete. Meanwhile, still watching the pennant, the Helmsman pulls the tiller (it is best to hold the tiller itself, rather than the extension, during this manoeuvre) towards himself and bears away *slightly*, just enough to bring the wind around to the same side as the mainsail. Then he shouts 'Gybe-ho!'.

This is the signal for the Crew to swing the boom across the boat with the kicking-strap. It is also the

signal for both crew-members to duck their heads, since the boom can give you a nasty bump.

While the boom is crossing in one direction, the Helmsman has to cross in the other. If the boat has a rear mainsheet system he faces backwards, so that he can hold onto the main sheet and tiller throughout the operation. If it has a central mainsheet it is more normal to face forwards. Whichever way he faces, however, he must be ready to take control of the boat as soon as the mainsail has been swung across. In the middle of the operation he must also swap the mainsheet and tiller from one hand to the other. This usually requires a certain amount of practice and the first few times you do it you may end up with everything in the wrong hand.

While the Helmsman is sorting out his affairs at the back of the boat, the Crew must be ready to move to either side to keep it on an even keel. He can let go of the boom as soon as it has crossed the centre of the boat, since the wind will take it the rest of the way of its own accord He should then re-adjust the jib which will not have been attended to since the beginning of the gybe.

With a little practice it should be possible to have the boat sailing normally two or three seconds after starting to gybe. However, it can still be a tricky operation in a strong wind and is probably the most frequent cause of a capsize, so it is best to master the technique in light winds first.

In squally winds, if possible, wait for a calmer moment before you gybe. At all events, do not try to gybe when you have just been struck by a gust, because it will be difficult, if not impossible, for the Crew to swing the mainsail across against the pressure of the wind. Try to keep the boat sailing straight while the boom is swinging across. If the boat starts luffing up before you have finished moving you may not have time to sit out and keep it upright. To counteract this, it is a good idea for the Helmsman to push the tiller back in the middle of the gybe to keep the boat sailing at 180 degrees to the wind. Don't overdo it, however, or you will end up gybing again in the opposite direction.

When sailing with the wind directly behind, even if not intending to gybe, the Helmsman should always keep an eye on the pennant. If it shows that the wind has come round to the same side of the boat as the mainsail, he should either push the tiller away to bring it back behind the boat at once or else gybe, because if he does not the boat may gybe unexpectedly of its own accord.

In a single-handed boat, where the Helmsman does not have a Crew to help him, he will have to swing the boom across himself. This can be done by hauling on the mainsheet, but he must release it as soon as the boom is across the middle of the boat to enable it to swing out on the other side.

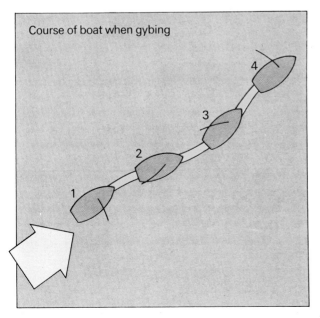

Course of boat when gybing

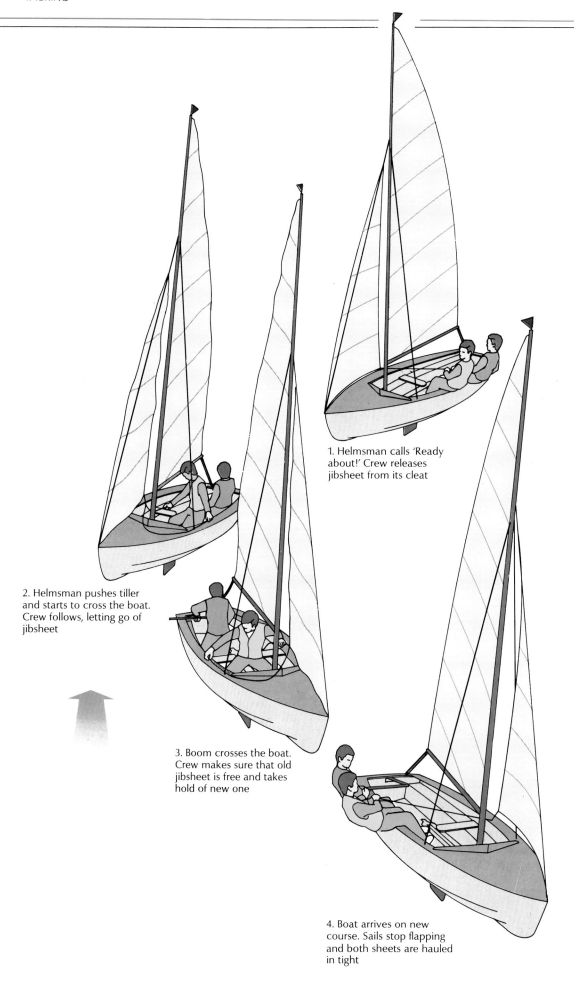

1. Helmsman calls 'Ready about!' Crew releases jibsheet from its cleat

2. Helmsman pushes tiller and starts to cross the boat. Crew follows, letting go of jibsheet

3. Boom crosses the boat. Crew makes sure that old jibsheet is free and takes hold of new one

4. Boat arrives on new course. Sails stop flapping and both sheets are hauled in tight

Tacking

'Tacking' means bringing the sails from one side of the boat to the other when the wind is directly *ahead*. This is also called 'going about'. Tacking and going about are the opposite of gybing, except that you can gybe without altering course at all, whereas tacking always involves turning through 90 degrees. This is because a boat cannot sail directly into the wind, but it can sail at angle of about 45 degrees to it, as we have seen. Tacking, therefore, involves turning through 45 degrees until the boat is pointing straight into the wind and then turning through a further 45 degrees until the boat is able to start sailing again.

During the tack the boat is not actually sailing and the sails just flap, instead of pushing it along. Consequently, before starting to tack, it is essential to have built up enough speed to keep the boat turning until it is sailing again. In light winds it is best to change course more slowly then in strong.

Before tacking the boat will normally be sailing along with the sails hauled in on one side and the Helmsman and Crew sitting on the other. The

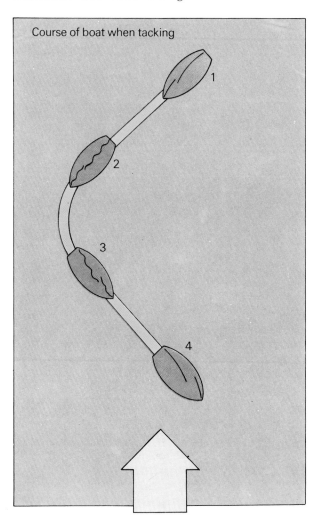

Course of boat when tacking

Helmsman usually warns the Crew that he is about to tack by shouting 'Ready about!'. At this point the Crew should jerk the jibsheet out of its cleat, but *not* release it yet, keeping it tight by hand. When the Crew is ready, the Helmsman shouts 'Lee-ho!' and pushes the tiller towards the opposite side of the boat.

Good tacking is, as much as anything else, a matter of balance. As soon as the sails start to flap the boat will stop heeling over and, if the Helmsman and Crew have not started to move across, they will end up sitting in the water. So they should time their movements to keep the boat more or less on an even keel throughout the manoeuvre. The Helmsman generally starts to cross as soon as he has moved the tiller, letting out the mainsheet slightly as he goes. The Crew waits until the boat has started to turn before he lets go of the jibsheet and follows the Helmsman across to the other side. The wind will take the boom across of its own accord when tacking, and so there is no need for the Crew to help it.

Because the boat has to turn through a full 90 degrees, Helmsman and Crew have much more time to organize themselves than they have when gybing. The Helmsman faces either forwards or backwards, as when gybing, and swaps the mainsheet and tiller from one hand to the other as he crosses the boat. The Crew faces forwards and takes hold of the other jibsheet, although he does not haul it in until the tack is complete. He should make sure that the original sheet is completely free, and if necessary he should pull it out through the fairlead, so that it will not interfere with the other sheet when that is hauled in.

As the boat arrives on the new course, both sheets are hauled in and the Helmsman returns the rudder to its normal position. At the same time both crew-members prepare to sit out if necessary, in order to keep the boat on an even keel.

Even in a strong wind tacking is a much less hazardous manoeuvre than gybing and there are not many ways in which you can come to grief. Nevertheless, a certain amount of practice will be necessary before you can do it perfectly. Many novice Helmsmen tend to 'overshoot' when tacking and end up sailing at about 90 degrees to the wind instead of 45. This loses a lot of ground when you are 'beating' against the wind (see page 65). A more dangerous situation may arise if the Crew delays too long before he lets go of the jibsheet. In strong winds, if you do not release it before the boat has finished tacking, a capsize may be the result. It is also important that the Crew does not haul in the new sheet too soon, because if the wind catches the jib on the wrong side the boat will be prevented from tacking and may start to turn back in the other direction.

Getting out of 'irons'

If the boat loses all speed when you are half-way through tacking, you will find that you are unable to make it turn any further or to make it turn back in the other direction. This situation is known as 'in irons' and it can be surprisingly difficult to get out of, unless you know the correct technique.

When the boat is not moving the rudder does not have any effect, and as long as the sails are flapping it is not possible to gather any speed either. However, the boat does not remain completely stationary for ever. Very soon the wind starts to push it backwards and, although it does not move very fast, the motion is enough to get the rudder working. It is then possible to make the boat turn by holding the rudder over to one side in the normal way. Bear in mind, however, that when it is moving backwards the rudder will make it turn in the opposite direction to what it would normally. In fact, the rudder works

rather like the front wheel of a bicycle and the back of the boat will follow in whichever direction you point it. In this way you can turn the boat until it is an angle of about 45 degrees to the wind, at which point you can sail away. The diagram shows the path of the boat during the course of this manoeuvre.

The jib, too, can be used to make the boat turn faster, as shown in the diagram. If you haul in the sheet so that the wind catches the sail on the opposite side to normal, it will push the front of the boat away from the wind. This technique known as 'backing the jib', is sometimes enough by itself to get a boat out of irons, and you do not have to wait until the boat is completely stationary before you use it. As we saw, backing the jib is something to be avoided when you are tacking normally, and when you are doing it on purpose you should let go of the jibsheet as soon as the boat is back on course.

When the boat is back at 45 degrees to the wind, you can straighten the rudder and, if it has been backed, haul in the jib on the correct side. Remember that as soon as the boat starts to move forwards again the rudder will start working normally and you will have to pull it in the other direction to make the boat turn further. Do not be in too much of a hurry to haul the mainsheet in again, because this may have the effect of making the boat turn straight back up into the wind. It is better to haul it in gradually as the boat gathers speed.

The most common reason for a boat getting into irons is that it is not travelling fast enough when the Helmsman begins to tack. This is particularly important when there is very little wind, and also when there are waves, which make a boat lose speed very rapidly. The same may happen if you try to tack twice in quick succession. If you have begun to tack and find that the boat does not have enough momentum, you should bear away onto your original course and build up more speed before trying again. If there are waves it is also worth waiting for a calmer patch before attempting to tack.

Boats which have a lot of weather helm are especially prone to getting into irons. Ways to reduce weather helm are described in Section 8, but the quickest method is to raise the centreboard slightly. (Do not raise it too much, however, or it will be impossible to steer the boat up into the wind at all.)

Although getting into irons is usually something which happens by accident, pointing the boat into the wind is a useful manoeuvre if you want to make some minor repair, for example, which cannot be done while the boat is sailing normally. Boats do not have brakes, so this is the only way to bring one to a halt without returning to land.

Opposite: Tacking. The tiller of the nearest dinghy has been pushed right over to make it tack as quickly as possible

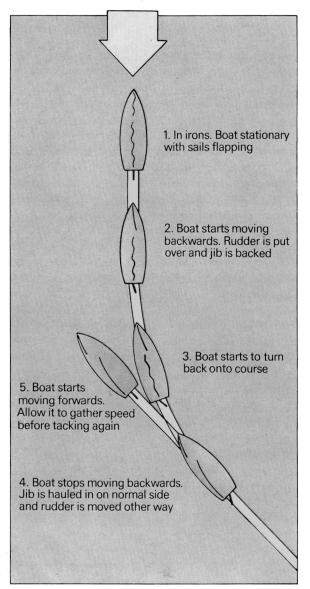

1. In irons. Boat stationary with sails flapping

2. Boat starts moving backwards. Rudder is put over and jib is backed

3. Boat starts to turn back onto course

5. Boat starts moving forwards. Allow it to gather speed before tacking again

4. Boat stops moving backwards. Jib is hauled in on normal side and rudder is moved other way

Beating into the wind

We have already said that a boat cannot sail directly into the wind. To be more precise, it cannot sail at an angle smaller than about 45 degrees to the wind direction. The exact size of this angle varies from boat to boat. A poorly designed boat may not be able to sail within 50 or 60 degrees, while a thoroughbred racing dinghy may be able to point rather closer than 45 degrees. But, in any case, there is an area enclosed within an angle of something in the region of 90 degrees which a boat cannot enter while sailing on one course. This is the 'No-go' area shown in the diagram below.

If you were at the centre of the circle, you could sail to any point within the blue area, simply by pointing the boat in the right direction and adjusting the sheets and centreboard accordingly. You could also sail to any point beyond the circle, provided it

was all in a straight line. However, if you tried to point the boat into the No-go area, the sails would start to flap and the boat would slow down and eventually stop. But this does not mean that any point within the No-go area is impossible to get to. All it means is that you cannot get to one by sailing on one course.

To get to a point within the No-go area you must sail a zig-zag course, sailing first at 45 degrees to the wind in one direction, then tacking and sailing at 45 degrees to the wind in the other. This process is called 'beating' and, in effect, it completes the circle by enabling you to reach all the points that you could not reach by sailing in a straight line. Of course, you do not always have to sail an equal distance on both courses. If your objective lies near the edge of the No-go area you will have to sail much further on one course than you will on the other.

It makes no difference how many 'zigs' and how many 'zags' you take (in other words, how many

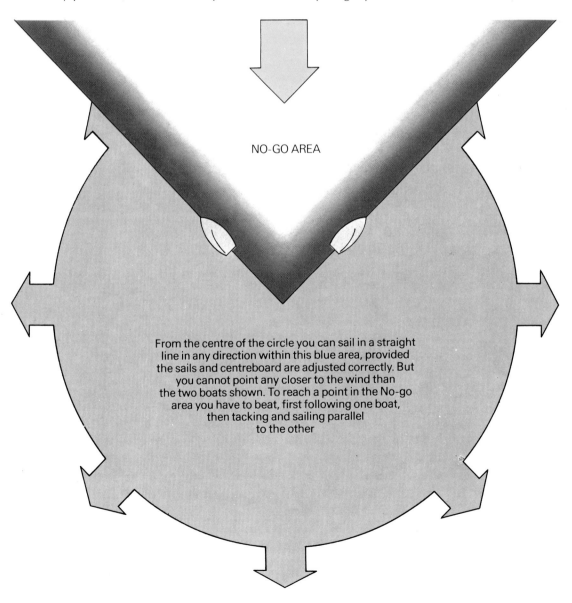

NO-GO AREA

From the centre of the circle you can sail in a straight
line in any direction within this blue area, provided
the sails and centreboard are adjusted correctly. But
you cannot point any closer to the wind than
the two boats shown. To reach a point in the No-go
area you have to beat, first following one boat,
then tacking and sailing parallel
to the other

times you tack) in order to reach your destination. You will get there just as fast and cover the same distance by doing a long stint in one direction, then tacking and doing a long stint in the other, as you will if you tack several times and do a lot of short zig-zags. The only possible disadvantage of trying to get there by tacking just once is that it may be difficult to judge when you have sailed far enough on the first course to be able to reach your destination on the other. Consequently, you may end up sailing further than necessary. On the other hand, every time you tack you lose speed temporarily and so if you tack *too* often you will take longer to cover the distance.

As a general rule, the closer that you can point towards your objective when beating, the quicker you will get there. This means sailing at as narrow an angle to the wind as possible, but do not try to narrow the angle so much that the sails begin to flap and the boat loses speed. The loss of speed may

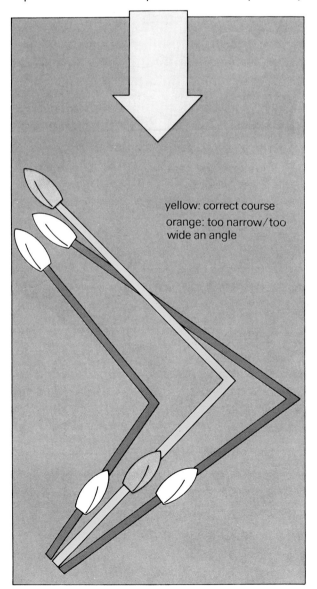

yellow: correct course
orange: too narrow/too wide an angle

not be noticeable at first, and you may think that you can gain a few degrees in the direction of your objective if the sails are flapping. What really happens is shown in the diagram on this page. The advantage of having less far to sail is more than cancelled out by the fact that the boat does not move as fast through the water.

The opposite mistake is to sail at too *wide* an angle to the wind. In this case the boat will move through the water quite fast and you may get the impression that you are outstripping boats which are sailing at a narrower angle to the wind. When you tack, however, you will find that you have gained less ground against the wind. The reason is that, although you have been travelling faster through the water, you have had to cover a greater distance.

The correct course lies mid-way between these two extremes. The diagram shows three boats setting out from the same point for a destination which lies directly upwind. The middle boat is sailing the correct course, while the left-hand one is pointing at too narrow an angle to the wind and the right-hand one at too wide an angle. After they have all sailed for the same length of time, it is the middle boat which is nearer to their destination. Notice that what counts when you are beating is not simply how far you can travel through the water in a certain time (as it is on other courses), but how much nearer you are to your destination.

An experienced sailor would tell you that there are certain times when you will reach your destination sooner by sailing at a slightly wider angle to the wind than normal. This depends partly on the type of boat you are sailing, but it is sometimes true when the water is slightly choppy. Under these conditions the extra speed will help the boat to push its way through the waves which would tend to slow it down if you were sailing at the normal angle. It is also true that there are certain times when it pays to steer the boat at a narrower angle than normal. This is known as 'pinching', and it may pay you to do so temporarily in order to squeeze past an obstruction, for instance, when you would waste more time by tacking.

Both these techniques, however, are only of interest to the experienced sailor (in particular to one who races) and you can safely ignore them when you have just started to sail.

The two boats in the diagram on the opposite page are sailing the course that you should try to steer when beating. It lies along the edge of the no-go area, which is really, of course, an invisible line. Keeping the boat pointing along it, so that, on the one hand, you do not cross into the no-go area and, on the other, you do not point at too wide an angle to the wind, requires a special technique which is explained on the next page.

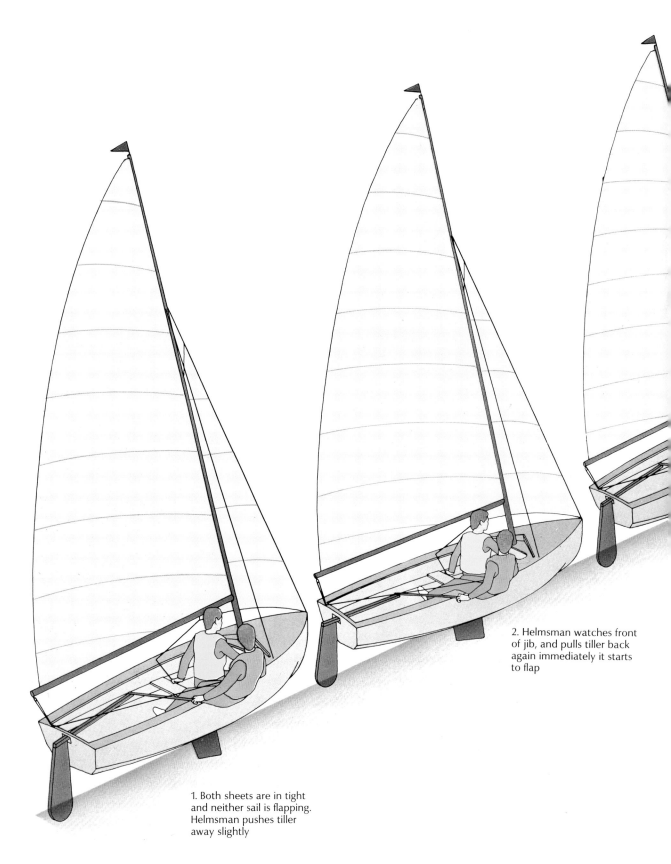

2. Helmsman watches front of jib, and pulls tiller back again immediately it starts to flap

1. Both sheets are in tight and neither sail is flapping. Helmsman pushes tiller away slightly

Steering the boat when beating

For beating, when you want to sail at as narrow an angle to the wind as possible, the sheets are hauled in and the centreboard is lowered to its fullest extent. On any other course if the sails started to flap you would haul in the sheets a bit further, until they had stopped flapping (see page 44). But when beating the sheets have already been hauled in as much as possible, so it is up to the Helmsman to stop them flapping, by altering course. He pulls the tiller towards himself and points the boat at a wider angle to the wind until the flapping stops.

It is easy enough to see when you are pointing at too *narrow* an angle to the wind because the flapping of the sails gives you warning of it. It is much less easy to see when you are sailing at too *wide* an angle to the wind (just as it is difficult to tell, at other times, that the sheets are hauled in too far) because the sails continue to look perfectly normal.

Once again, trial and error is the best method. You point the boat slowly up into the wind, watching the area of the sails about a third of the way up. When a slight fluttering appears near the leading edge you know that you have gone too far. Pull the tiller back towards you *slightly* and you will then be on the correct course.

The more often that you repeat this procedure the better, because you can then be sure that you are sailing as near to the wind as possible the whole time. You should only have to move the tiller a very small amount, so little, in fact, that a casual observer might not notice that the boat was changing course at all. After a bit of practice it will become second nature, and a good Helmsman can steer a perfect course almost without thinking about it.

Theoretically, both sails should begin to flap at exactly the same time. In practice, however, it is best to watch the leading edge of the jib because this gives the best indication of when you are sailing at too narrow an angle to the wind. Make sure that the sheet is hauled in far enough, or else you may not be pointing as close to the wind as you can. Sometimes you will find that the trailing edge (the leach) of the sails will flap even when you are sailing correctly. This is usually just a sign that the sails are old, or badly made, and you can ignore it.

When you are beating, the Crew has less to do than the Helmsman. He still has to help keep the boat on an even keel, but there is nothing to do with the jibsheet or the centreboard. However, while the Helmsman is busy watching the sails he has less time to look around him, and so the Crew should keep a special look-out for other boats which the Helmsman may need to avoid.

4. Boat is now sailing at as narrow an angle to the wind as possible. Helmsman starts to repeat operation

3. Immediately the jib stops flapping, Helmsman returns tiller to normal position

6. Getting Under Way and Returning to Land

The Crew of the boat in the foreground is holding it pointing into the wind.
K 387 has just got under way. The wind is blowing away from the shore, so this is a fairly straightforward operation

There are no hard and fast rules for getting under way or returning to shore, since the best strategy depends partly on the geography of the beach or landing-stage that you are dealing with. However, with a bit of common sense, the procedures shown on the next few pages can be adapted to any situation.

Before you can get under way the sails must be hoisted. This is usually done by the Helmsman, while the Crew holds the boat pointing towards the wind. Never try to hoist them with the wind behind (the same applies when you are lowering them), and make sure that the sheets are free to run out; otherwise, the boat will try to sail away or may get blown over. Hoist the sails by hauling on the halyards where they come out of the bottom of the mast. The jib luff should be tighter than the forestay, and it may help if the Crew pulls forwards on the forestay while you are tying the halyard around the cleat. As you hoist the mainsail you must feed the bolt-rope into the bottom of the groove on the mast, as you did with the boom. When it is up, fit the boom onto the gooseneck and tighten the kicking-strap. Coil up the ends of the halyards neatly after they have been cleated. Then mount the rudder, and you are ready to sail away.

If the wind is blowing towards the shore at an angle, set off on whichever course takes you away from the shore quickest, like the boat on the left in the diagram below.

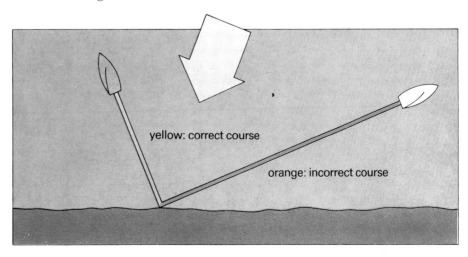

yellow: correct course

orange: incorrect course

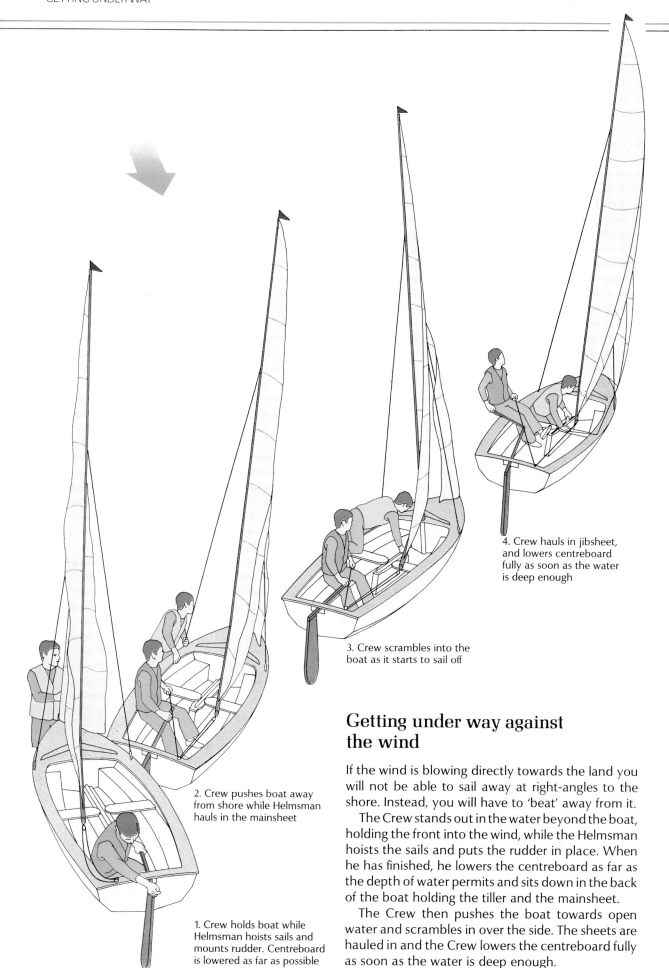

4. Crew hauls in jibsheet,
and lowers centreboard
fully as soon as the water
is deep enough

3. Crew scrambles into the
boat as it starts to sail off

2. Crew pushes boat away
from shore while Helmsman
hauls in the mainsheet

1. Crew holds boat while
Helmsman hoists sails and
mounts rudder. Centreboard
is lowered as far as possible

Getting under way against the wind

If the wind is blowing directly towards the land you will not be able to sail away at right-angles to the shore. Instead, you will have to 'beat' away from it.

The Crew stands out in the water beyond the boat, holding the front into the wind, while the Helmsman hoists the sails and puts the rudder in place. When he has finished, he lowers the centreboard as far as the depth of water permits and sits down in the back of the boat holding the tiller and the mainsheet.

The Crew then pushes the boat towards open water and scrambles in over the side. The sheets are hauled in and the Crew lowers the centreboard fully as soon as the water is deep enough.

Getting under way with the wind behind

When the wind is blowing away from the shore getting under way is an easier matter than when it is blowing towards it.

As before, the Crew holds the boat pointing towards the wind while the Helmsman hoists the sails and mounts the rudder. When the Helmsman has settled himself in the boat, the Crew works his way towards the back of it, holding on as he goes, and allowing it to swing round until it is pointing away from the land. As the boat starts moving forwards, he scrambles over the side. Once aboard, he adjusts the jibsheet as necessary.

3. Crew adjusts the jibsheet

2. Crew turns boat away from shore and scrambles aboard as it moves off

1. Crew holds onto boat, while Helmsman hoists sails and mounts rudder

1. Boat approaches shore sailing at a narrow angle to the wind until water starts getting shallow

2. Helmsman pushes tiller. Crew releases jibsheet and raises centreboard partly

3. Helmsman points boat straight into wind and releases mainsheet. Crew prepares to jump over the side when the water is shallow enough

4. Crew holds boat pointing into wind while Helmsman lowers the mainsail

Returning to land against the wind

Just as it was a comparatively simple matter to get under way when the wind was blowing off the shore, so it is relatively easy to return to land under these circumstances. The main problem when coming to land, whether it is the wall of a quay or a shelving beach, is in slowing the boat down so that you do not damage it by running into the shore. Ideally the boat should have lost all momentum at exactly the moment when the Crew can grab the quay or the water is shallow enough for him to jump overboard and hold onto the forestay. The Helmsman manages this by gradually pointing the boat up into the eye of the wind so that the sails begin to flap and the boat loses speed. You can slow down more by releasing the sheets so that the sails flap even before you start pointing into the wind. The boat will not stop immediately, so it is best to start easing the sails when you are still some way from land and approach as slowly as possible. You can always pick up speed, if necessary, by hauling in the sheets again.

Returning to land with the wind behind

Coming to land with the wind behind you is more complicated than doing so against the wind. It is not possible to make the mainsail flap when the wind is behind the boat, but if you approach the shore with the mainsail full of wind it may be difficult to stop. The wisest course is for the Helmsman to steer the boat up into the wind and for the Crew to lower the mainsail while you are still some distance away from the shore. You can then sail slowly towards land with the jib only. At the last minute the Crew releases the jib sheet and jumps into the water or grabs the quay. As before, the Crew holds onto the front of the boat while the Helmsman removes the rudder. The jib may be lowered now or left hoisted until the boat is on shore.

1. Boat approaches shore with the wind behind. Crew prepares to lower mainsail

2. Helmsman points boat straight into the wind. Crew lowers the mainsail as quickly as possible

3. Boat continues slowly towards the shore with only the jib hoisted

4. Helmsman points boat into the wind again. Crew jumps out and holds onto front

7. Handling the Boat on land

When you have finished sailing for the day the boat is usually taken out of the water and stored on land. The vast majority of dinghies are kept in dinghy parks which are in easy reach of the water. These may belong to sailing clubs, or they may be an area set aside for the purpose by the local authorities. In either case, a small charge is generally made for leaving a boat there, and if the park belongs to a sailing club you will have to be a member.

It is worth taking care of your boat and seeing that it is put away properly at the end of each sailing expedition. The temptation may be, if you have got wet and are beginning to feel a bit cold, to finish the job as quickly as possible and go away to get warm. In this situation it is probably best to get changed first, then come back and finish tidying up the boat.

Large boats are normally kept in the water, attached to permanent 'moorings' or in 'berths' in a marina. Heavier dinghies, too, are sometimes kept on moorings, although they have to be in places which are well sheltered from wind and waves. It is important to visit the boat periodically, if you are not sailing very often, to make sure that it has not filled up with rainwater or spray. The disadvantage of keeping a boat on a mooring is that it does not get much chance to dry out, but this is less of a problem with glass-fibre boats than wooden ones.

If you are only going to be on land for an hour or two it may be possible to leave the boat alongside a quay or landing-stage. You should take down the sails and put the rudder away in the bottom of the boat. Mooring ropes should not be too tight, to allow for the rise and fall of the waves. Make sure that the boat cannot come to any harm, or do any damage to others. Even if the water is calm, the waves caused by a passing vessel may throw it against the quay or boats tied up nearby.

It is unwise to leave a dinghy in the water unattended for very long. Ideally, you should be there to keep an eye on it the whole time. A better plan, if you have to leave it, is to haul it just out of the water, provided there is not a rising tide.

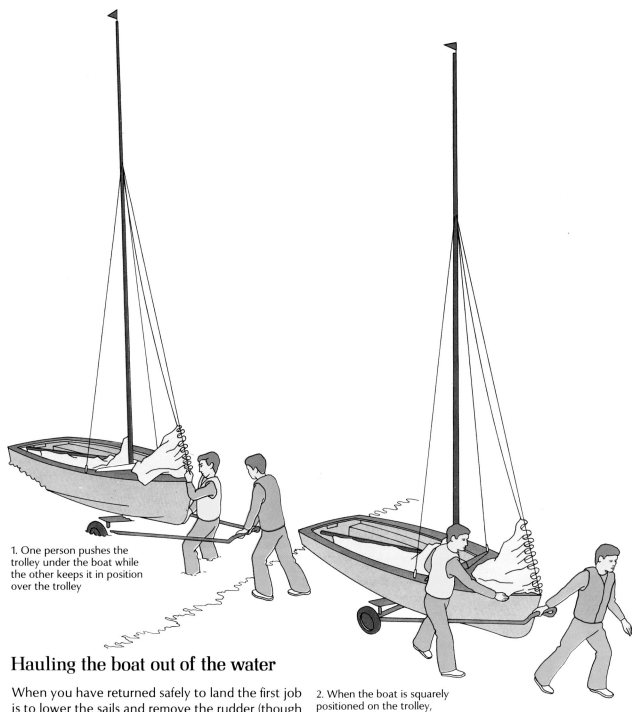

1. One person pushes the trolley under the boat while the other keeps it in position over the trolley

2. When the boat is squarely positioned on the trolley, it is pulled out of the water

Hauling the boat out of the water

When you have returned safely to land the first job is to lower the sails and remove the rudder (though you may prefer to leave the jib hoisted until the boat is out of the water). Then, while one person holds the boat, the other goes to get the launching trolley.

The procedure for hauling the boat out of the water is really just the reverse of that for launching. The boat is swung round until it is pointing towards the shore. One person lifts up the front while the second pushes the trolley underneath it. Alternatively, if the water is deep enough, you can push the trolley in until it is sufficiently submerged for the boat to be simply floated onto it. In either case, make sure that the boat is squarely positioned on the trolley as it comes out of the water. If it is off-centre,

one of the pads may be digging into the bottom and could make a hole.

Once the boat is out of the water, it is taken to the dinghy park or other destination. As before, try not to let the bottom scrape along the ground, by keeping it evenly balanced on the trolley. If you find it rather hard work hauling the boat uphill, there will probably be no shortage of people willing to help you, provided, of course, that you give them a hand with their boats when the time comes.

Folding up the sails

Although some people just cram their sails away into a bag without bothering to fold them at the end of a day's sailing, it is much better to fold them up carefully. Modern terylene or dacron sailcloth is much stiffer than the cotton which sails used to be made of, and it will last much longer if it does not get crumpled up. It only takes a few moments to fold a sail correctly.

The way to fold up the mainsail is as follows. Take out the battens and remove the sail from the boat. Starting at the bottom, fold the sail backwards and forwards so that the folds run from the front to the back with about 50 centimetres (18 inches) between each fold. When you have reached the top, the pile should be roughly rectangular in shape. Now fold it lengthways until you have a neat bundle.

The jib is folded slightly differently because there is a wire running up the front of the sail which may get kinked if you bend it too sharply. Roll the sail up from top to bottom as if you were coiling the luff wire like a rope. Smooth out any creases in the sail as you go. When you reach the bottom, roll it up lengthways, so that the coiled wire is in the middle.

It is easiest to fold both sails by spreading them out on the ground first, but you must be careful that they do not get mud or grass stains on them if you do it this way. It may be a better idea to fold them up on the foredeck of the boat.

When the sails have been folded they usually go into a sailbag. This is normally made of the same material as the sails and has a draw-string to close the opening. You can put the battens in the bag, too, but be careful that they are kept straight (especially if they are wood), or they may acquire a permanent bend. It may be better to store them flat in the bottom of the boat. But (again if they are wood) it must be dry or they will get warped.

If either of your sails has a 'window' (a transparent panel so you can see to the other side), this should not be folded sharply because the crease may not come out when the sail is hoisted again. You should also avoid folding any part of a sail again and again in the same place, for this reason. If your sails do become creased, do not iron them. In time, the creases will disappear.

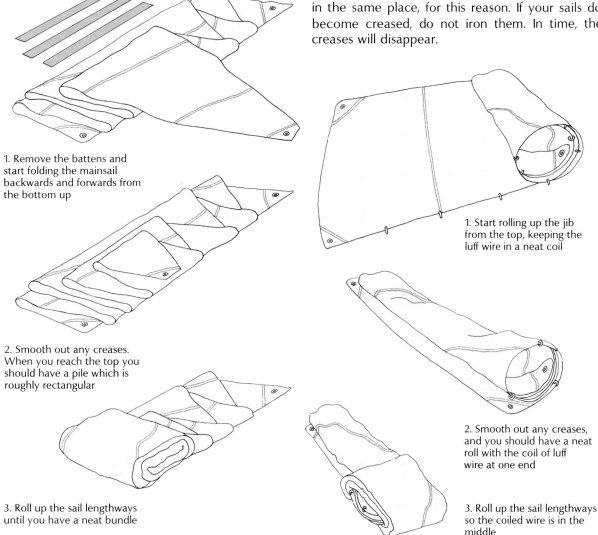

1. Remove the battens and start folding the mainsail backwards and forwards from the bottom up

2. Smooth out any creases. When you reach the top you should have a pile which is roughly rectangular

3. Roll up the sail lengthways until you have a neat bundle

1. Start rolling up the jib from the top, keeping the luff wire in a neat coil

2. Smooth out any creases, and you should have a neat roll with the coil of luff wire at one end

3. Roll up the sail lengthways so the coiled wire is in the middle

Putting the boat away on land

When the sails have been folded up, the boat is ready to be 'put to bed'. Normally, it will be left on the trolley, but this should be pulled out a little so that the back of the boat is resting firmly on the ground. Open the drainholes, or 'transom-flaps' if the boat has them, to let out any water that has collected, and leave them open to let out the rainwater that gets in. If it is a wooden boat, you should sponge out inaccessible corners where water is left, to stop rot forming. Hatchcovers, if the boat has them, should be left open to permit air to circulate through them.

Rudders are usually stored inside the boat. They should be laid on a flat surface to stop them getting warped. The sails may be left in the boat as well.

A lightweight dinghy can sometimes be blown over by a strong wind, if it is parked in an exposed position. To prevent this, you can tie a rope (the jibsheet may do) around the mast and attach either end to a concrete block or a peg stuck into the ground beside the boat.

To protect the boat from the weather, and to discourage pilfering, it is a good idea to have a boat cover, made out of canvas or plastic. These are available to fit most common classes of dinghy. But, if you cannot find one that fits, it is easy enough to have a cover specially made. They usually lace up round the mast and have two or three ties that pass underneath the boat. The best ones are of the 'boom-up' variety, as shown here. These covers fit over the boom when it is on the gooseneck, forming a ridge down which the rain can run off.

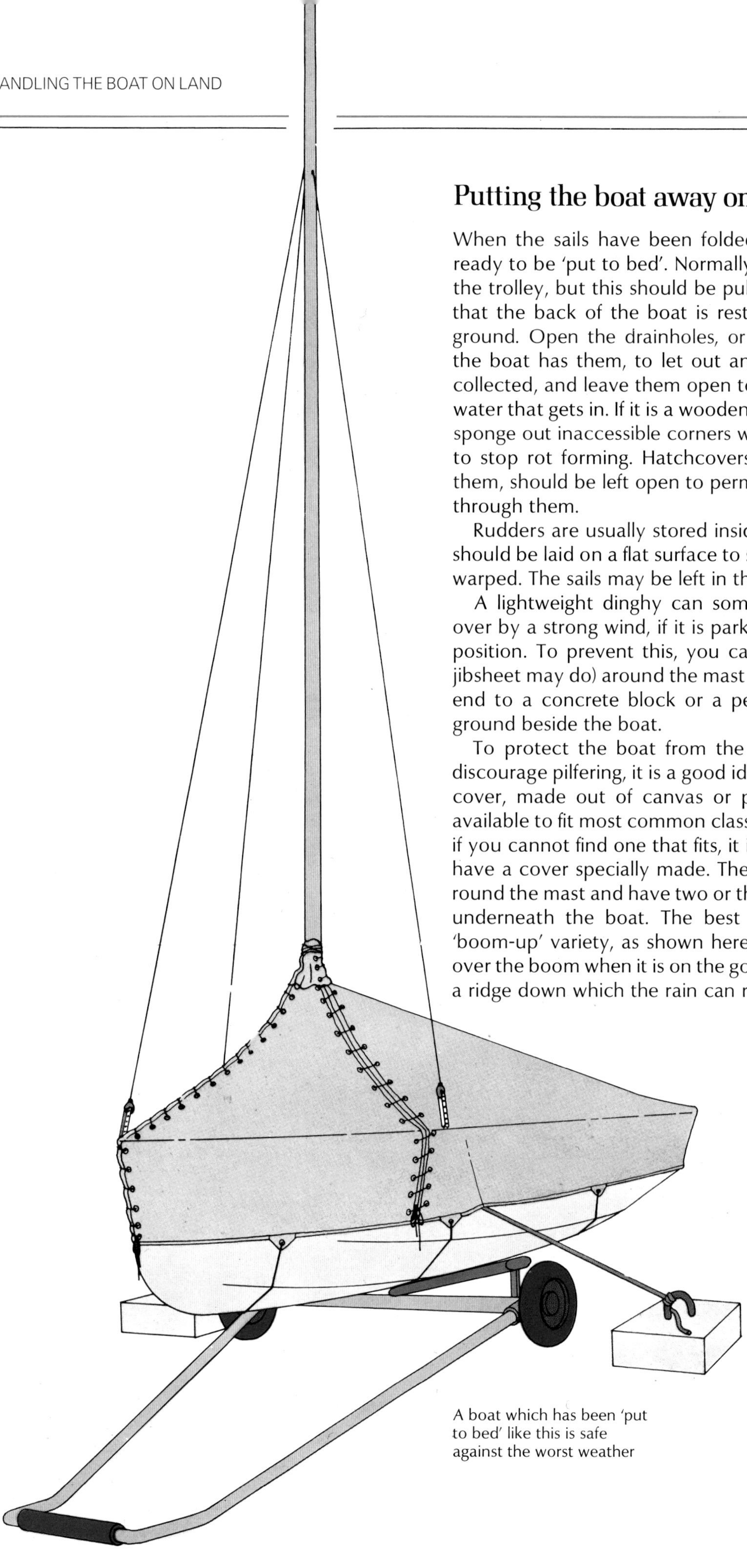

A boat which has been 'put to bed' like this is safe against the worst weather

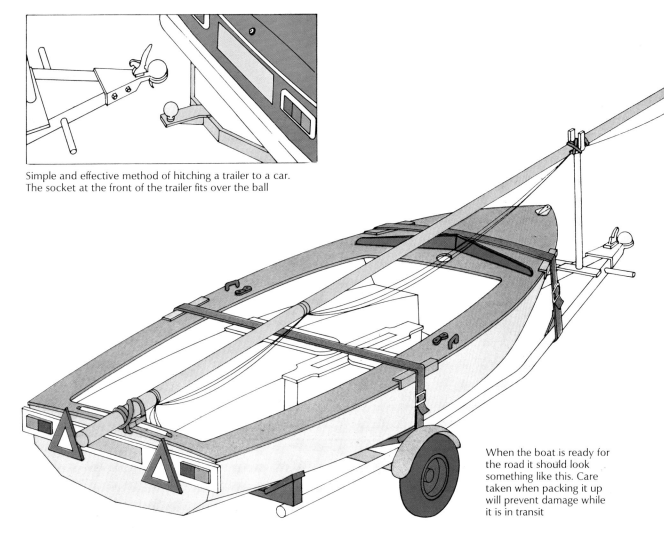

Simple and effective method of hitching a trailer to a car. The socket at the front of the trailer fits over the ball

When the boat is ready for the road it should look something like this. Care taken when packing it up will prevent damage while it is in transit

Moving the boat by road

From time to time you may want to move your boat to another stretch of water by road. To do so you will need a properly built boat trailer. Once again, there are trailers available to fit most common classes of dinghy, and there are also adjustable ones which can be adapted to fit most shapes of boat of a certain size.

Almost all cars are perfectly capable of towing an average dinghy. (Some people even tow them behind large motorcycle-sidecar combinations.) The car will need to be fitted with a towing hitch (a 'ball-hitch' is the most usual type), and a correctly wired-up socket for the lights. The legal requirements for towing vary from country to country and you should check on them before you start, but you are generally required to have a number plate and a full set of lights on the back of the boat. They can all be mounted on a board which is attached to the rudder mountings.

A dinghy's mast is longer than the boat itself and so there is usually a special support at the front of the trailer, to hold the end of the mast above the roof of the car. Alternatively, the support can be fitted on the boat itself, where the mast would be normally.

Needless to say, the boat must be securely tied down onto the trailer. Any point at which it is in contact with the trailer should be well padded. The vibrations caused when the car is travelling at speed can cause damage to the bottom of the boat if it is rubbing against a hard surface. Some people also put a cover around the bottom of the boat to prevent damage from stones and chippings thrown up by the wheels. The mast should also be securely attached, at two points at least, and padded to stop wear.

You should make sure that any equipment, such as the rudder and tiller, which is carried loose in the bottom of the boat cannot slide around. It may be necessary to tie it down, or carry it inside the car.

When the boat has been loaded up, the centre of gravity of the trailer should be slightly in front of the wheels. If it is too far back it will tend to lift the back wheels of the car off the road.

8. Expert Boat Handling

So far we have only been concerned with the basic controls of a sailing boat—sails, centreboard, crew weight and rudder. Even if your boat has other pieces of equipment you have not needed them until now. This is because the basic controls are the only essentials for making a boat sail, and the techniques of using them might be called the 'basic skills' of sailing. When you start sailing it is usually wise to limit yourself to mastering these basic skills. However, if you are interested in becoming more than just competent at sailing, the time will come when you will want to use some of the other pieces of equipment and 'secondary controls', which are not actually necessary to make the boat sail, but which will make it sail faster and more efficiently. And by increasing your skill you will increase your enjoyment as well.

The first part of this section deals with the secondary controls. These are used to modify the shape of the sails to suit different strengths of wind. The same shape of sail is not ideal for all wind strengths, but by using these secondary controls you can pull or push the sails into whatever shape is best for the conditions. The second part of the section is concerned with the 'trapeze'. This piece of equipment enables the Crew to support his entire weight over the side of the boat and make it a much more effective counterweight to the force of the wind against the sails. Trapezing is as spectacular as the term suggests. Lastly we come to the spinnaker. This large, balloon-shaped, usually brightly coloured sail greatly increases the boat's speed when sailing at wide angles to the wind. On other courses it is lowered and stowed away. Spinnaker work calls for careful handling and quick reactions, but sailing fast under a billowing spinnaker is one of the most thrilling experiences that sailing has to offer.

Not all boats have the equipment described in this section. It may be possible to fit it, though if you are intending to use your boat for racing you should see what equipment the rules of the class allow. It is not, however, generally possible to fit a trapeze or spinnaker to a boat which is not designed for one.

Using the secondary controls

Seen from the side, sails look flat, but if you could view the boat from above you would see that they are really curved, rather like a cross-section of an aeroplane's wing. (In fact, they both work on the same principle.) The curve is most pronounced near the front of the sail and it flattens out towards the back. This is the shape that experience has shown to be most efficient at using the power of the wind. The

sailmaker achieves it by tapering the seams between the pieces of cloth that make up the sail.

Although this shape is much more effective than a mere flat surface would be, it does not work equally well in all strengths of wind. A slightly different shape to what is best for light winds will make the boat go faster when the wind is strong. The sailmaker will usually make a sail that is somewhere between the two extremes, and suitable for winds of medium strength. But by pulling or pushing the 'secondary controls' you can vary the shape of the sail to suit conditions of more or less wind.

As a rule, a fairly flat sail is best for strong winds, and one with the most pronounced curve quite near the leading edge. For light winds the sail can have a bit more 'fullness' and it should curve more evenly throughout its length. There is no need to go into the reason why one or other shape is best for a particular wind. All you need to know is how to obtain the right shape.

The shape of the sails makes most difference when you are sailing at a narrow angle to the wind or beating. And it is with this in mind that you adjust the sails before you start sailing. When sailing at wider angles to the wind a slightly different shape is sometimes preferable, and so some of the controls should be re-adjusted when you alter course.

The shape of the jib is affected by three controls: the tightness of the halyard, the position of the fairlead and the tightness of the sheet. The mainsail is controlled by four things: the 'Cunningham hole',

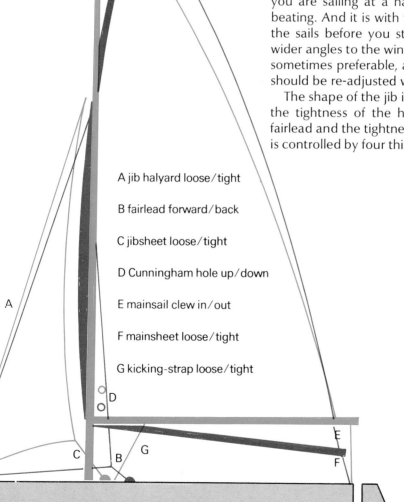

A jib halyard loose/tight

B fairlead forward/back

C jibsheet loose/tight

D Cunningham hole up/down

E mainsail clew in/out

F mainsheet loose/tight

G kicking-strap loose/tight

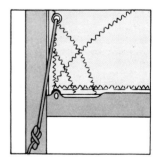

Leave the Cuningham hole control line slack in light winds on all courses

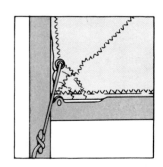

Tighten the control line in stronger winds to pull the Cunningham hole down

the distance that the clew is pulled out along the boom, the tightness of the sheet and the tightness of the kicking-strap. Of course, the main purpose of the sheets is to control the angle of the sails. But the last few centimetres, if they are hauled in as far as possible, makes more difference to the shape of the sail than to their angle.

Jib halyard The jib halyard controls the tension along the luff of the sail. In light winds it should not be pulled too tight, just tight enough to make the luff tighter than the forestay. In stronger winds it should be pulled very tight, so that it takes all the strain off the forestay. As we have mentioned already, a good way to do this is for the Crew to pull forwards on the forestay while the Helmsman is tightening the halyard.

Fairlead position Some jib fairleads are mounted on

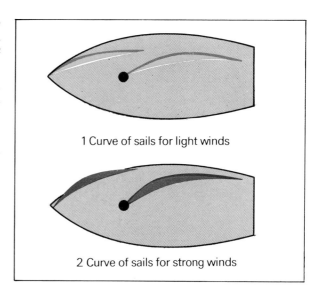

1 Curve of sails for light winds

2 Curve of sails for strong winds

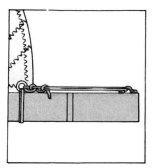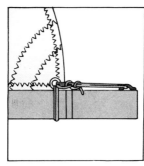

In light winds pull the mainsail along the boom enough to remove the creases

In stronger winds pull the bottom of the sail as tight as possible

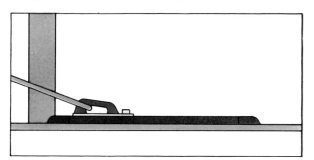

For light winds move the jibsheet fairlead forward and do not haul the jibsheet in too tightly, when sailing at a narrow angle to the wind or beating against the wind

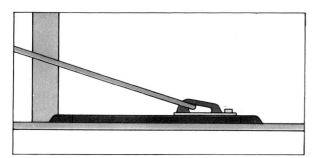

In strong winds move the fairlead back when sailing at a narrow angle to the wind, and haul the jibsheet very tight. Move the fairlead forward again on any other course

a track so that they can be moved backwards or forwards. If your's can be moved, they should be pushed forwards for light winds and back for stronger winds. This changes the angle at which the sheet pulls downwards on the sail. A similar effect is achieved on some boats by moving the sail up or down a few centimetres at the tack. The fairlead should always be moved forwards when sailing at wide angles to the wind, however, in any conditions.

Jibsheet Tightening the jibsheet makes the sail flatter. It should not be too tight in light winds, but should be hauled in more or less as tightly as possible when the wind is strong.

Cunningham hole Pulling downwards on the Cunningham hole near the tack of the mainsail has the same effect as tightening the halyard did on the jib. For light wind sailing it can be left untouched, but in stronger winds it should be pulled down towards the boom a centimetre or two using the control line. At wide angles to the wind the control line should be released.

Mainsail clew By not pulling the clew of the mainsail out to its fullest extent when you are putting it on the boom you allow more curvature or fullness in the sail for light winds. In stronger winds the bottom of the sail should be stretched along the boom as tightly as possible.

Mainsheet As with the jib, the sheet should not be hauled in as tightly when sailing at a narrow angle to the wind, or beating, in light conditions as it is in strong winds.

Kicking-strap Tightening the kicking-strap pulls the boom downwards, which has the effect of bending the top of the mast backwards and flattening the sail. In light winds the kicking-strap should not be too tight. In stronger winds it should be tightened by hauling in the mainsheet as far as possible, when the boat is pointing into the wind, and taking up the resulting slack.

Changing the angle of the mast

We mentioned earlier that excessive weather helm could be cured by raising the centreboard slightly. A more satisfactory and permanent solution is to alter the angle, or 'rake', of the mast.

Excessive weather helm, or lee helm, makes the boat difficult to steer. It also slows it down, because the fact that the rudder is always at an angle to the direction in which the boat is sailing has the effect of a brake on the flow of water. A small amount of weather helm may be acceptable, or even desirable, but keeping it within bounds will make the boat easier to handle and will improve the 'feel' of the tiller for the Helmsman.

To lessen weather helm you should make the mast lean further forwards. To lessen lee helm you do the opposite. The amount of weather or lee helm is determined by the position of the centre of sidewards force against the sails relative to the centre of sidewards resistance in the centreboard. In other words, the boat pivots around the centreboard, and when there is a larger area of sail towards the back of the boat than there is at the front of the boat to balance it, the front of the boat will get pushed towards the wind (i.e. you will experience weather helm). When there is more sail area in front of the centreboard, the opposite will be true.

When you half-raise the centreboard it swings backwards, moving the centre of resistance towards the back of the boat. This is why you can combat weather helm by raising the centreboard. With a dagger-board, which only moves up and down, the centre of resistance does not move, so you cannot achieve the same effect.

As you can see from the diagram, the amount that you need to alter the rake of the mast in order

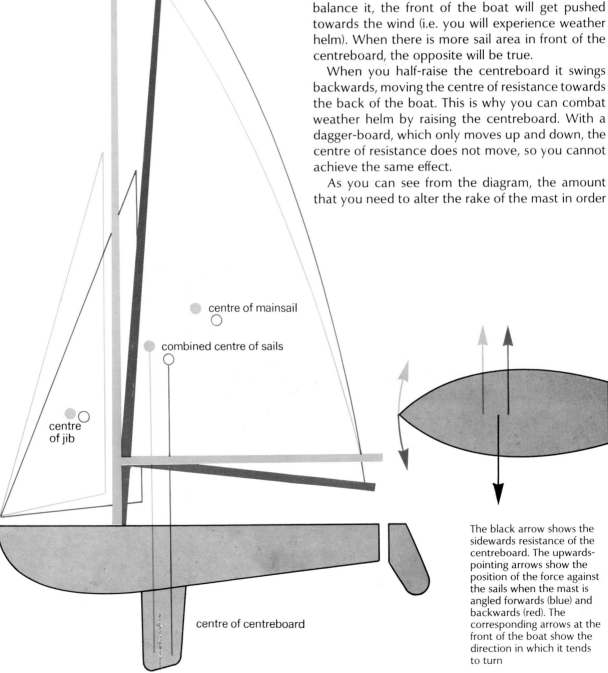

centre of mainsail

combined centre of sails

centre of jib

centre of centreboard

The black arrow shows the sidewards resistance of the centreboard. The upwards-pointing arrows show the position of the force against the sails when the mast is angled forwards (blue) and backwards (red). The corresponding arrows at the front of the boat show the direction in which it tends to turn to affect weather helm is very small. So make any adjustments with caution. All that you have to do is to tighten or loosen the forestay a centimetre or two, and adjust the side-stays accordingly. Of course, this can only be done while the boat is on land, and it is only on the water that you can find out whether it has had the desired effect. So a certain amount of trial and error may be required before you get it right. You may also find that the effect varies according to wind strength. (Using different sails can also make a difference.) In that case, you should make a note of the correct adjustment for particular conditions, so that you can find it again whenever they occur.

Effect of moving the mainsheet traveller out for strong winds (in red), and in for light winds (in blue)

Effect of letting a central mainsheet traveller out, to ease the pressure of the wind in strong gusts

Using the mainsheet track

This is another control system that can be adjusted to suit strong or light winds, provided that the slide, or 'traveller', is fitted with control lines which enable you to position it where you want.

The same principles apply with both rear and centre mainsheet arrangements. The normal position for the traveller, to which the lower mainsheet block is attached, in light winds is the middle of the boat. When sailing at a narrow angle to the wind the sheet is not hauled in very tightly under these conditions, and so the boom is free to swing out at a slight angle to the centre of the boat. In strong winds the sheet should be hauled in as tightly as possible, but at the same time you do not want to have the boom parallel to the centre of the boat. The solution is to allow the traveller to run to the far end of the track. If you release the control line at the other end, too, the traveller will cross of its own accord to the other end of the track when you tack. Of course, in winds of medium strength it is not necessary to let the traveller right out to the end of the track, and it should only be let out part of the way.

Sometimes, rear-mounted mainsheet tracks do not have control lines, but moveable stops instead. These, when set at the appropriate point in the track, have the same effect. Other boats do not have fixed tracks at all, but the block is free to travel along a length of rope which is attached on either side. Tightening or loosening this rope has the effect of letting the traveller move nearer to the end of the track or keeping it in the middle.

There is another technique, which can only be used with a central mainsheet system, for making the boat go faster in strong winds. Under normal circumstances, when both crew-members are already sitting out, you would release the mainsheet to ease the pressure of the wind against the sail if a gust struck it. This would keep the boat on an even keel, but it means that the sheet is no longer helping to make the mainsail flat, which slows the boat down. With a centre system you do not have to release the mainsheet at all, unless the gust is a very strong one. Leaving the sheet itself in its cleat, you release the control line, allowing the traveller to run to the opposite end of the track. This will reduce the boat's tendency to heel, but at the same time keep the mainsail the right shape for strong winds.

When beating against the wind with a centre mainsheet track you can often leave the mainsheet cleared the whole time, and simply 'play' the traveller backwards and forwards to keep the boat on an even keel. However, it is wise to release the sheet when you tack, and it should always be to hand so that in an emergency you can release it as well as the traveller.

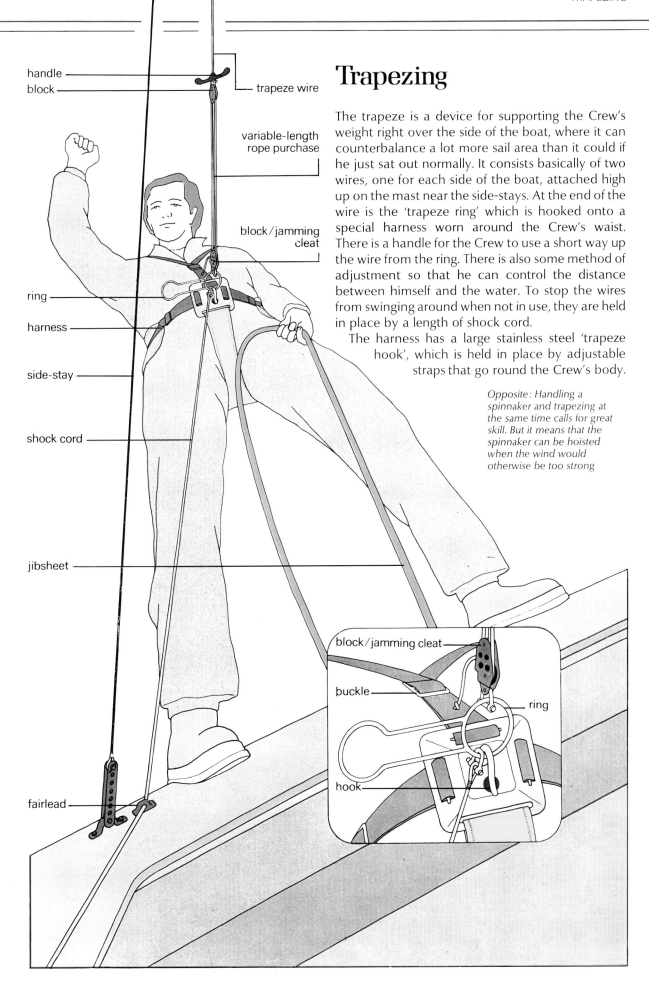

handle
block
trapeze wire

variable-length
rope purchase

block/jamming
cleat

ring

harness

side-stay

shock cord

jibsheet

fairlead

block/jamming cleat

buckle

ring

hook

Trapezing

The trapeze is a device for supporting the Crew's weight right over the side of the boat, where it can counterbalance a lot more sail area than it could if he just sat out normally. It consists basically of two wires, one for each side of the boat, attached high up on the mast near the side-stays. At the end of the wire is the 'trapeze ring' which is hooked onto a special harness worn around the Crew's waist. There is a handle for the Crew to use a short way up the wire from the ring. There is also some method of adjustment so that he can control the distance between himself and the water. To stop the wires from swinging around when not in use, they are held in place by a length of shock cord.

The harness has a large stainless steel 'trapeze hook', which is held in place by adjustable straps that go round the Crew's body.

Opposite: Handling a spinnaker and trapezing at the same time calls for great skill. But it means that the spinnaker can be hoisted when the wind would otherwise be too strong

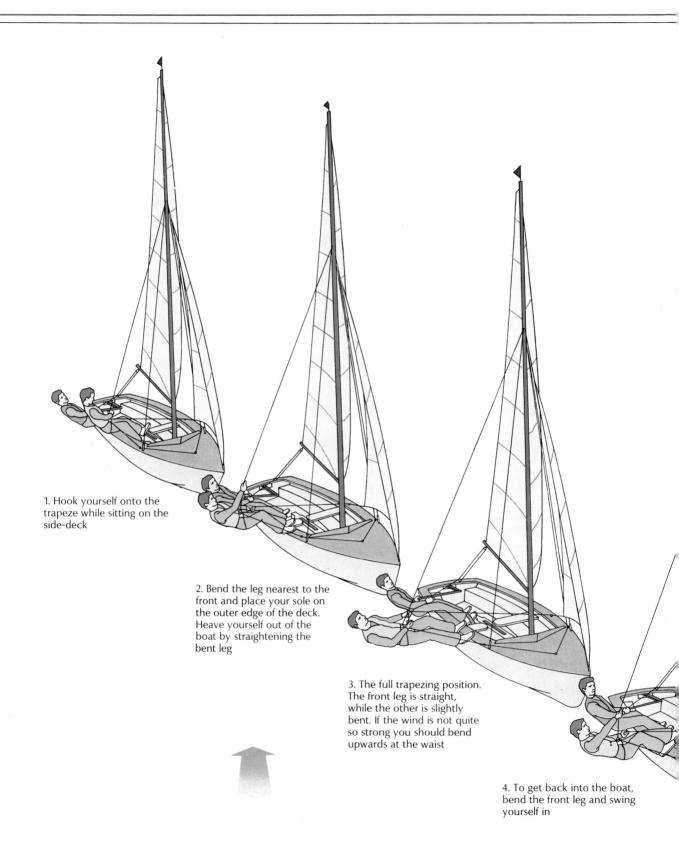

1. Hook yourself onto the trapeze while sitting on the side-deck

2. Bend the leg nearest to the front and place your sole on the outer edge of the deck. Heave yourself out of the boat by straightening the bent leg

3. The full trapezing position. The front leg is straight, while the other is slightly bent. If the wind is not quite so strong you should bend upwards at the waist

4. To get back into the boat, bend the front leg and swing yourself in

Using the trapeze

Trapezing is not a difficult operation, and the trapezing position is so comfortable and gives you such a spectacular view that you will never want to sail on a boat without a trapeze, once you have tried it.

It is important that the harness is put on tightly enough before you start. The hook should be slightly below the waist, so that you are suspended more or less at the body's centre of gravity. The trapeze should support you in a roughly horizontal position, parallel to the surface of the water when the boat is upright, and the height of both rings should be adjusted accordingly. A common fault is to have the ring too high, so that the body is at an angle to the water, in which position your weight has less leverage over the boat.

Before you attempt to use the trapeze the wind should be fairly steady and there should be no major alteration of course immediately ahead. Sitting on the side-deck, you hook yourself onto the trapeze ring. Bend the leg which is nearest your instep on the outside edge of the side-deck. Steady yourself by holding onto the handle. Now heave your whole body out onto the trapeze by straightening the leg.

In the normal trapezing position your front leg should be more or less rigid, while you lean your body slightly towards the back of the boat by bending the other one at the knee. The flexing of the bent leg will absorb any shocks caused by the boat ploughing into waves, and will stop you swinging round the front of the mast and landing in the jib, which sometimes happens to beginners. To get the full benefit of the trapeze you should straighten your body at the waist, and real 'professionals' fold their hands behind their heads during gusts.

To get yourself back into the boat, just bend the front leg again and swing the other one in over the side-deck. Gravity will help you, and you can also pull on the jibsheet, which you should hold even when trapezing.

Confidence plays a large part in successful trapezing. At first you may not be able to convince yourself that such a thin wire could support your weight. But don't worry, it can! You also need to have confidence that your Helmsman will not let you be deposited in the water, so you should only trapeze with an experienced Helmsman. It is also unwise to try trapezing when the wind is variable, in strength or direction, which rules out waters that are overshadowed by trees or buildings.

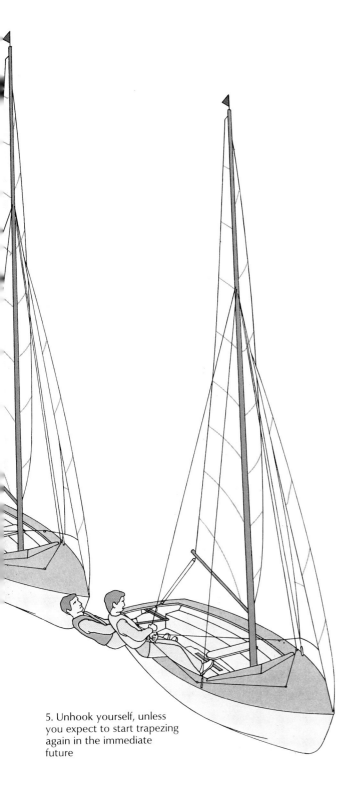

5. Unhook yourself, unless you expect to start trapezing again in the immediate future

Sailing with a spinnaker

A spinnaker is a large, balloon-like sail which is hoisted only when you are sailing at a wide angle to the wind. At other times it is lowered and put away. With experience, you will be able to use a spinnaker even when sailing at right-angles to the wind. But at first you should only attempt to hoist it when the wind is more or less directly behind the boat.

Unlike the other sails, the spinnaker is symmetrical in shape, so it can be hoisted either way round. Because it has to be hoisted while the boat is sailing along, the sail and all its equipment is designed for quick assembly. Most racing dinghies have a 'spinnaker chute', a long tube with an opening near the forestay into which the sail is pulled when not wanted. A more traditional system is to lower the sail into the cockpit, where it is stored in a bag fixed to rear edge of the foredeck, beside the mast.

The area of the spinnaker may be greater than that of the jib and mainsail put together, so the extra speed that it gives the boat is considerable. It also demands a fair amount of skill, and teamwork, from both Crew and Helmsman. Normally, the jib is left up when the spinnaker is hoisted. However, for reasons of clarity, the jib is not shown in the drawings on the following pages.

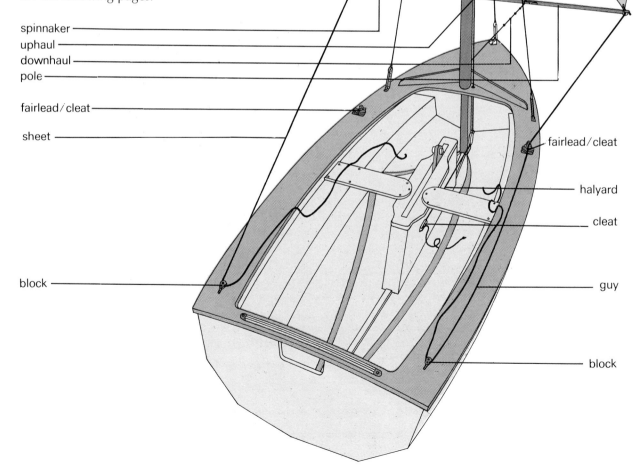

spinnaker
uphaul
downhaul
pole
fairlead / cleat
sheet
block

fairlead / cleat
halyard
cleat
guy
block

Spinnaker equipment

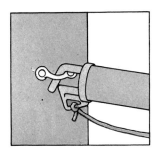

Method of attaching pole to mast. The clip can be opened by pulling the line

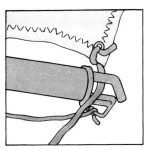

At the other end the pole is clipped around the Guy near the sail

Spinnaker halyard runs around a block on the mast above the forestay

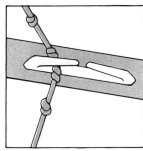

Clip on middle of pole for uphaul-downhaul. It can be used either way round

The Sheet is hooked under a special fairlead when it becomes the Guy

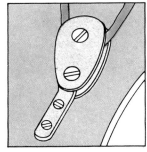

Each spinnaker sheet runs round a block near the back of the boat

Apart from the sail itself, you will need various other pieces of equipment and fittings before you can use a spinnaker. The exact nature and number of the fittings, and their lay-out, can vary quite a lot.

The most important piece of equipment is the spinnaker pole. This is usually made out of a length of alloy tubing with a special quick-release clip at either end. The clips are designed to fit onto a ring on the side of the mast, at one end, and around the spinnaker sheet where it is attached to the sail, at the other. Both ends of the pole are the same, and it can be used either way around. When the spinnaker is hoisted the pole should be horizontal, so that the corner of the sail is at the same height as the ring on the mast. (The corners should also be roughly at the same height as one another.)

The pole is held horizontal by means of an adjustable length of rope, or shock cord, called the 'uphaul-downhaul'. This begins near the base of the mast and is attached to the mast at a roughly equal distance above the ring. In between, it passes through a special type of clip on the middle of the pole, and it is usually knotted at intervals to stop the pole slipping upwards or downwards.

The spinnaker has its own halyard which comes off the mast just above the top of the forestay (unlike the jib halyard which emerges just below it). The halyard may be tied to the top of the spinnaker, but a better method is to use some sort of lightweight clip that can be easily undone. (It is useful to have similar clips on the end of the sheets.) On most dinghies the spinnaker halyard runs round a block and down the outside of the mast, then through the foredeck, round another block in the bottom of the boat, finally being led back to the Helmsman, who has the job of hoisting it when the time comes. After hoisting, the end of the halyard is held in a quick-release cleat, so that it can be lowered again quickly.

The spinnaker has two identical sheets, one on either side. But, unlike the jibsheets, both are used at the same time. Terminology can be confusing here, because each one is called both the 'Sheet' and the 'Guy' at different times. It is called the Sheet when it is attached to the free corner of the sail and the Guy when it is attached to the corner which is held by the pole. From the corners of the sail the sheets are led to the back of the boat, where they go round a pulley wheel, and then back to the Crew who controls them. There is often a special fairlead and jamming cleat for the Guy in front of where the Crew sits. The fairlead is designed so that the Guy can be released from it when it becomes the Sheet during gybing.

When the spinnaker is lowered, it is pulled into the cockpit, either just behind or just in front of the side-stay on the opposite side to the spinnaker pole. The pole itself is removed from the mast *and* the sheet, and carried loose in the bottom of the boat. The sheets should be left attached to the sail, so the Guy will be running round the outside of the forestay and into the boat on the other side. The halyard, too, may be left attached, or it may be removed from the sail. In the second case, it should be attached to some convenient point, such as the base of the stay, so that the end cannot disappear up the mast, from where it would be impossible to retrieve.

In this state the spinnaker is ready to be hoisted again. But it is wise to check that it has not become twisted, or else it may go up in a tangle.

Although for clarity it is not shown opposite, the ends of both sheets are normally passed round another block at the side of the cockpit, facing the Crew. This keeps them out of the Helmsman's way, and they can be cleated there when gybing.

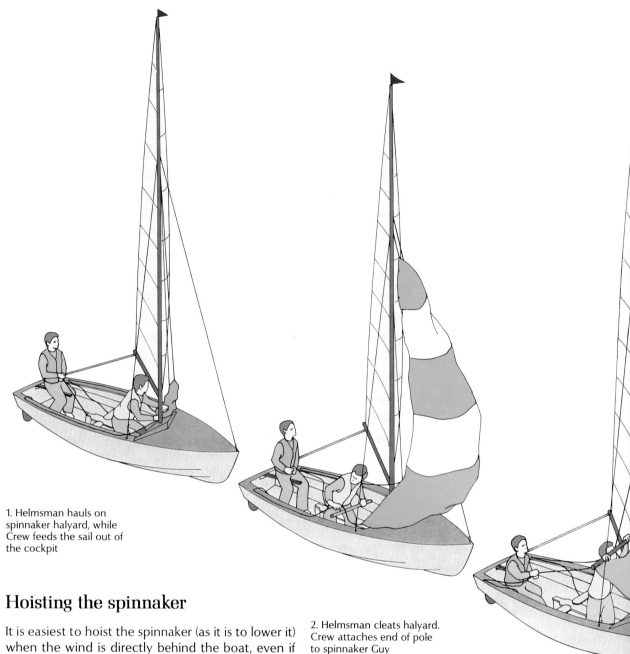

1. Helmsman hauls on
spinnaker halyard, while
Crew feeds the sail out of
the cockpit

2. Helmsman cleats halyard.
Crew attaches end of pole
to spinnaker Guy

3. Crew fixes pole to mast
and attaches uphaul-
downhaul. Helmsman hauls
in Guy

Hoisting the spinnaker

It is easiest to hoist the spinnaker (as it is to lower it)
when the wind is directly behind the boat, even if
that means altering course slightly while the job is
done. It should be hoisted on the same side as the
boom because then it will be sheltered by the mainsail until it is up.

If it happens to have been lowered on the other
side, previously, you should take the sheets off the
sail and tie their ends together, along with the end of
the halyard. Then pass the whole lot round the front
of the boat and re-attach them to the spinnaker on
the right side.

When you are ready to hoist, the Helmsman
stands up in the back of the boat, facing forwards
and steering with the tiller between his knees. He
pulls the halyard while the Crew gradually feeds the
sail out of the cockpit, under the boom and between
the side-stay and the mast. When the sail has been
hoisted to the top of the forestay the helmsman

cleats the halyard, while the Crew picks up the spinnaker pole.

The Helmsman pulls the spinnaker round in front of the boat with the Guy, until it begins to catch the wind. The Crew attaches the pole, first to the Guy, near the corner of the sail, then to the mast, attaching the uphaul-downhaul as he does so. The Helmsman may continue to hold the Guy while the Crew gets hold of the Sheet and hauls it until the sail is drawing properly. The Guy can then be cleated and the Helmsman resumes sailing normally.

The whole operation is best attempted for the first time in a very light wind. Otherwise, the wind may take charge of the sail before you have got it fully under control. When you are more experienced you need have no qualms about hoisting the spinnaker in much windier conditions. But there will always be a limit to the amount of wind in which you can safely use a spinnaker, which depends partly on its size and the type of boat that you are sailing.

When you are going to be hoisting a spinnaker for the first time it is also a good idea to fold it up neatly on land before you set out. It should be rolled into a loose bundle with the three corners projecting from it.

4. Crew pulls in Sheet until spinnaker is drawing properly

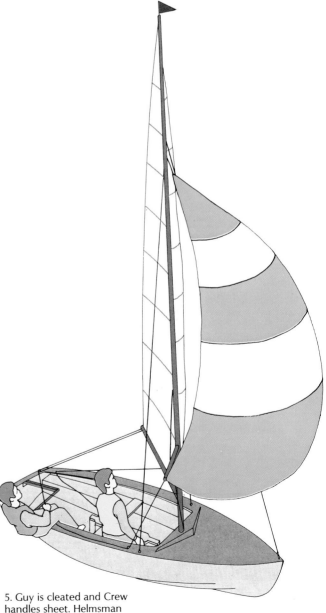

5. Guy is cleated and Crew handles sheet. Helmsman sits out, if necessary, to keep boat upright

93

Playing the spinnaker

'Playing' the spinnaker means adjusting and re-adjusting the Sheet so that the sail is always at the right angle to the wind. The spinnaker is extremely sensitive to quite small variations in course or wind direction. This is most marked when the wind is not directly behind, but at an angle to your course. Under these conditions the Crew will have to concentrate quite hard to keep the Sheet correctly adjusted at all times.

While the Crew is playing the spinnaker he is controlling more than half the boat's total sail area, so he must be in a position where he has a good view. This means that the Helmsman must take more of the responsibility for keeping the boat on an even keel. If necessary he should even sit on the same side as the mainsail and steer while looking under the boom at what is going on ahead.

The Crew has the Guy as well as the Sheet to think about. Fortunately, the Guy does not require such regular attention and need not normally be adjusted unless there is a fairly substantial change in the boat's course relative to the wind. The rule for the Guy is that the spinnaker pole should be roughly at right-angles to the wind direction (until it comes up against the forestay, when it should not be let out any further).

The procedure for playing the spinnaker is basically the same as that for adjusting the other two sails. Let the Sheet out gradually until you have gone *just* too far. This will be seen by watching the edge of the sail about half way up. When this edge begins to curl inwards, breaking the curved outline of the sail, the Sheet is out too far. Pull it in again quickly until the curl disappears and the curve is restored, sometimes with an audible sound.

You may find that you have to pull the Sheet in quite a long way, in which case you should let it out again *immediately* to almost the same extent, because it will otherwise be too far in. But the sooner you notice that the edge has begun to curl, the less far you will have to haul the Sheet in.

1. Spinnaker is drawing normally. Let the Sheet out gradually

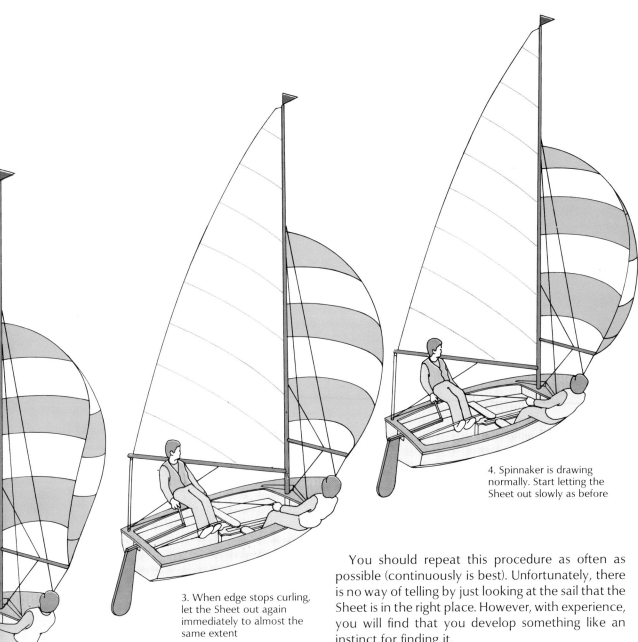

2. When leading edge begins to curl, haul the Sheet in

3. When edge stops curling, let the Sheet out again immediately to almost the same extent

4. Spinnaker is drawing normally. Start letting the Sheet out slowly as before

You should repeat this procedure as often as possible (continuously is best). Unfortunately, there is no way of telling by just looking at the sail that the Sheet is in the right place. However, with experience, you will find that you develop something like an instinct for finding it.

If you allow the edge of the spinnaker to curl too much the sail will 'collapse'. You will soon recognize this state of affairs when you see it. The spinnaker resembles a punctured balloon and flaps violently. In order to rectify it you will have to haul the Sheet in a long way. The Helmsman may even have to make the boat bear away. *Immediately* the sail is drawing again, let the sheet out, as before.

If the spinnaker Sheet is pulled too far in, the boat may develop violent weather helm, and it could capsize if the Crew does not act quickly. Even when the Sheet is properly adjusted you must be prepared to release it, and let the spinnaker collapse, if the boat cannot be kept upright.

Gybing the spinnaker

Gybing with the spinnaker up is more difficult than gybing normally, because you have the spinnaker to think about in addition to the usual matters. The simplest approach is to cleat the Sheet and the Guy while you carry out the rest of the operation, even if the spinnaker collapses in the meantime.

Once the boom has been swung across the boat the Crew can turn his attention to the spinnaker. He should unclip the pole from the mast and attach it to what was formerly the Sheet, but is now the Guy.

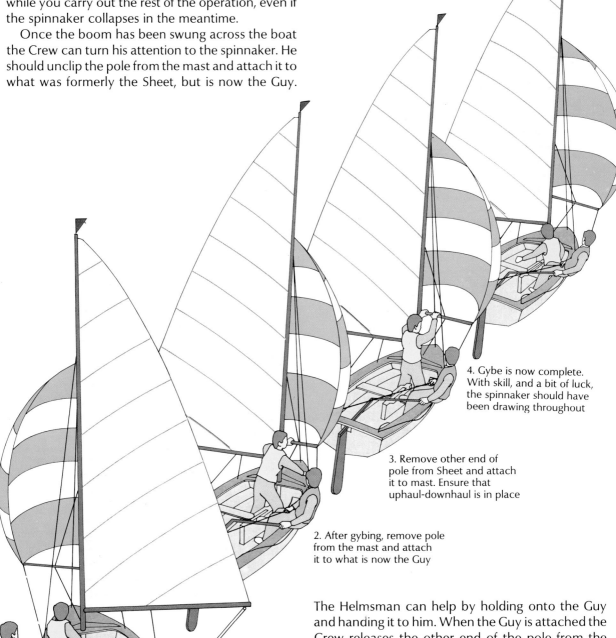

4. Gybe is now complete. With skill, and a bit of luck, the spinnaker should have been drawing throughout

3. Remove other end of pole from Sheet and attach it to mast. Ensure that uphaul-downhaul is in place

2. After gybing, remove pole from the mast and attach it to what is now the Guy

1. Before gybing, cleat the Sheet and the Guy. Prepare to gybe in the normal way

The Helmsman can help by holding onto the Guy and handing it to him. When the Guy is attached the Crew releases the other end of the pole from the original Guy (now the Sheet) and clips it onto the mast. The uphaul-downhaul should remain attached to the pole throughout the operation. If not, the Crew must re-attach it. All that remains to be done is to re-adjust the Sheet and the Guy for the new course.

Like gybing under any conditions, gybing with a spinnaker is easiest to do if the boat is kept on a course with the wind behind until the operation is complete.

Lowering the spinnaker

The first step in lowering the spinnaker is for the Crew to unclip the pole at both ends and put it away in the bottom of the boat. The Sheet is released so that the spinnaker collapses, and the Crew takes hold of the Sheet underneath the boom, at a point as near to the corner of the sail as possible.

At this moment the Helmsman releases the Guy, making sure that it is free to run out. Now the Crew works his way quickly along the sheet until he can grasp the corner of the sail, and then along the bottom of it until he has both corners in his hands. When the Crew is ready, the Helmsman releases the spinnaker halyard and lets it down *slowly* so that the Crew has time to gather the sail into the boat.

If the spinnaker is allowed to fall into the water while it is being lowered, and the boat is moving fast, it may be dragged out of the Crew's hands. A submerged spinnaker is extremely difficult to retrieve, and it also places a severe strain on the mast.

Unlike the other sails, the spinnaker is made of a cloth that will come to no harm if it is crumpled up But, as we have seen, it may be a good idea to sort it out roughly, to make hoisting easier next time.

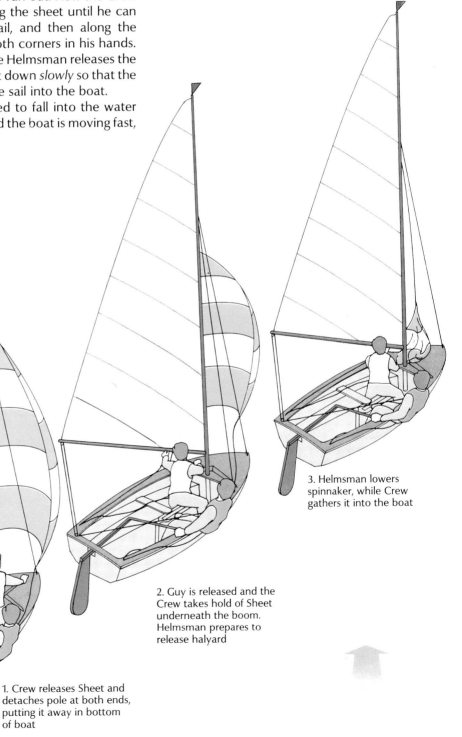

3. Helmsman lowers spinnaker, while Crew gathers it into the boat

2. Guy is released and the Crew takes hold of Sheet underneath the boom. Helmsman prepares to release halyard

1. Crew releases Sheet and detaches pole at both ends, putting it away in bottom of boat

9. Sailing in Stronger Winds

Sailing in a strong wind tests the skill of both crew-members. The Helmsman and Crew of this 'Enterprise' dinghy are managing to keep it dead upright in spite of the conditions. At such times the feeling of speed is even greater than the boat's speed itself. Notice how the mast is bending

For your first attempt at sailing it is sensible to choose a day when the wind is not too strong. Reactions do not have to be so quick when the wind is light, and you do not have to be very concerned about the possibility of capsizing the boat. The same applies when you are trying out any new manoeuvre on the water. Nevertheless, you do not want to pick a day of total calm. You cannot learn about the effect of the wind on the sails when you cannot tell which way the wind is blowing. A wind of about Force 2 on the scale on the next page gives ideal conditions for the beginner.

When you have begun to master the basic manoeuvres, you will probably want to try something a little more testing. And it is when you are ready to try your skills in a wind of Force 4 or more that sailing becomes most thrilling. But you should not necessarily wait until you feel that you are experienced enough to set sail deliberately in those conditions, before you begin to study the techniques of sailing in stronger winds. On the sea, especially, the wind can build up quite rapidly, and you may find yourself having to cope with a Force 4 not long after setting out in a gentle Force 2. But a competent sailor can deal with winds much stronger than Force 4.

As a rule, you should make all course alterations more slowly in a strong wind, and pay particular attention to keeping the boat as upright as possible at every stage. Do not hesitate to let the mainsail flap in order to keep the boat on an even keel, and the jib, too, if necessary. However, surprisingly enough, most capsizes happen when the wind is behind the boat. Some mistakes to avoid are described on pages 102 and 103. Gybing can be tricky in a strong wind, but if the worst comes to the worst you can sail round in a complete circle and tack instead. You can reduce your sail area, before setting out, by 'reefing'. This can also be a useful technique when you first start to sail in light winds, since it makes the boat much easier to handle.

Sailing in stronger winds is not just a matter of taking precautions. It is also the time when most modern dinghies will 'plane', reaching much higher speeds than many larger boats. Tearing down the face of a wave, leaving a wake like a destroyer, is one of the most exciting experiences that any sport has to offer.

Preparing for strong winds

Before you decide to go sailing you should always study the weather conditions. The most important consideration for a sailor is the strength of the wind. On land the wind is often less strong than it is out on the water, especially at sea. You should learn to judge the wind strength by looking at the surface of the water and the behaviour of other boats. In this way you will know what to expect when you have set sail, whether to reef, and whether you have enough experience to deal with the conditions.

The sailor's usual system for describing the strength of wind is in terms of the Forces of the Beaufort scale, shown in the table below. The original scale goes up to Force 12, but the dinghy sailor is highly unlikely to be interested in anything more than Force 7. And most sailors would stay on land in winds considerably less than that.

The second column of the table gives the wind speed in knots. However, more often than not there is no way of measuring the speed of the wind, and so you normally judge the Force by the descriptions in the next column. The Beaufort Scale proper is concerned with conditions in the open sea. Dinghy sailors usually keep to more enclosed waters where

waves do not build up to the same extent, even in strong winds. You must make an allowance for this when you come to judge the wind force. To help you, the descriptions have been modified to give an idea of the appearance of inland waters, as well as the open sea. But there can still be quite a big difference between large and small expanses of water inland.

The fourth column tells you the sort of sailing conditions which you are likely to meet in winds of a given Force. Most dinghy sailing is done in winds between Force 1 and Force 4. Force 4 and above can be counted as a strong wind, almost certainly requiring you to reef the mainsail unless you have sailed in such conditions several times before. Anything stronger than Force 4 is only suitable for experienced sailors, and capsizing may become a common occurrence, even for them. In the open sea the size of the waves would make dinghy sailing extremely hazardous, but in sheltered waters the experts may still be sailing in Force 6.

Even though you may not capsize, dinghy sailing is always a wet sport in winds of Force 4 and above. If there are waves there will be plenty of flying spray. As well as a lifejacket, you will probably need a waterproof outer garment, top and bottom. If the water is cold it is not only more comfortable, but safer to wear a 'wet suit' of the kind that skin divers wear, which keeps you warm whether it is wet or dry.

FORCE	WIND SPEED IN KNOTS	DESCRIPTION	SAILING CONDITIONS
0	0	Flat calm. Surface like a mirror	Sailing boats make no progress
1	1–3	Small ripples on the surface. Wind can be felt on the face	Sailing boats make slow progress and do not heel. Helmsman and Crew sit on opposite sides
2	4–6	Surface still calm, but small waves begin to form. Leaves move in the wind	Good conditions for the beginner. Dinghies move more briskly and begin to heel
3	7–10	Small waves. Crests break occasionally. Wavelets on inland waters. Branches in leaf begin to sway	Excellent sailing conditions. Some sitting-out required. Dinghies begin to plane at wide angles to the wind
4	11–16	Medium waves. Crests break fairly regularly. Waves form on inland waters	Exciting conditions for the more experienced. Beginners should reef. Most dinghies plane at high speed
5	17–21	Larger waves. Crests break frequently. Sea becoming rough. Some breaking waves even on inland waters	Testing conditions even for the more experienced dinghy sailor. Not recommended for beginners
6	22–27	Large waves with white breaking crests Sea rough. Waves break regularly on open waters inland	Only suitable for expert sailors. Dinghies can only be kept upright by allowing the mainsail to flap
7	28–33	Open sea becoming very rough. Breaking waves even in enclosed waters	Not suitable for dinghy sailing

Making the mainsail smaller

'Reefing is a way of making the mainsail smaller so that the boat is easier to sail, especially in strong winds. There are two basic methods.

The usual modern way to reef a sail is 'roller-reefing'. This means rolling the lower part of the sail around the boom as it is hoisted. The technique is quite simple and can be used on almost any boat. The only part of the operation requiring special care is making sure that the sail is rolled neatly, so that it does not spoil the remaining part of the sail by causing creases.

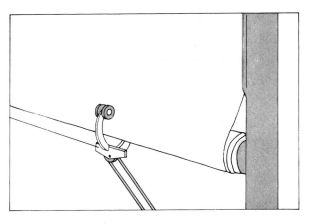

Reefing claw, used to attach the kicking-strap to the boom when roller-reefing. A rope or wire attached to the end of the boom stops it sliding up to the mast

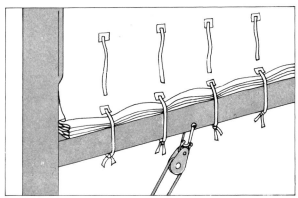

Reef-point method of reefing the mainsail. A second row of reef-points is provided for reducing the sail area even further. The kicking-strap is attached in the normal way

If a mainsail is roller-reefed the kicking-strap cannot be attached to the boom in the normal way. Instead, it is attached to a 'reefing claw' which fits around the boom, on top of the rolled-up sail. To stop the claw being pulled along the boom to the mast, where the kicking-strap would have no effect, it must be connected to the end of the boom by a length of rope or wire. If the mainsheet is attached to the middle of the boom, you will need a claw for that as well.

The more traditional method of reefing is by 'reefing points'. These are short lengths of thin rope which pass through the sail and are sewn onto it in rows. To reef a sail by this method you simply bunch up the bottom on top of the boom and tie the reefing points around either side. With this system there are no problems with the kicking-strap, but you can only reduce the sail as much or as little as the rows of reefing points permit.

There is no easy way to reduce the size of the jib, but some boats have a smaller one that can be substituted for the normal jib in strong winds. The jib itself cannot be reefed.

Sailing with a roller-reefed mainsail. A smaller jib can also be used in strong winds

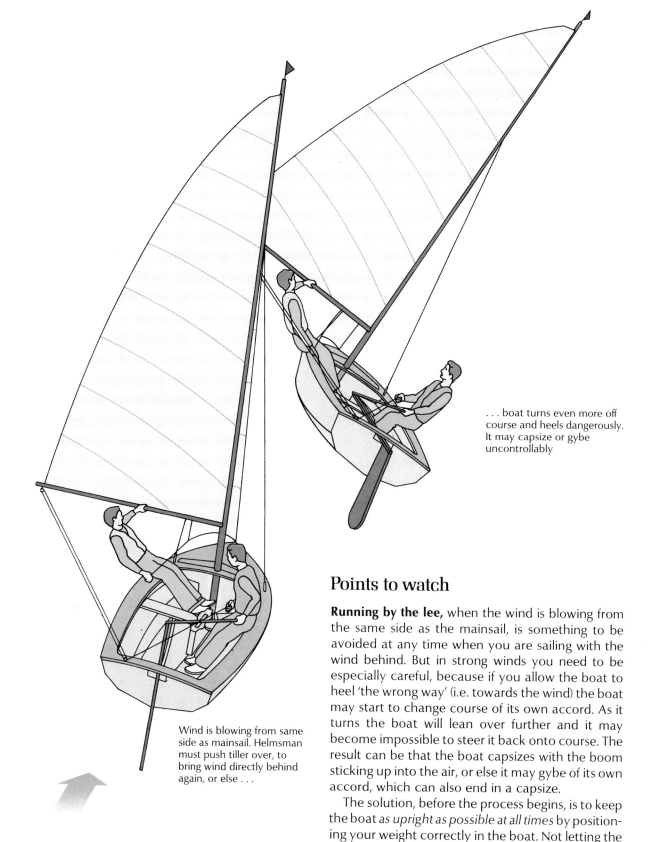

. . . boat turns even more off course and heels dangerously. It may capsize or gybe uncontrollably

Wind is blowing from same side as mainsail. Helmsman must push tiller over, to bring wind directly behind again, or else . . .

Points to watch

Running by the lee, when the wind is blowing from the same side as the mainsail, is something to be avoided at any time when you are sailing with the wind behind. But in strong winds you need to be especially careful, because if you allow the boat to heel 'the wrong way' (i.e. towards the wind) the boat may start to change course of its own accord. As it turns the boat will lean over further and it may become impossible to steer it back onto course. The result can be that the boat capsizes with the boom sticking up into the air, or else it may gybe of its own accord, which can also end in a capsize.

The solution, before the process begins, is to keep the boat *as upright as possible at all times* by positioning your weight correctly in the boat. Not letting the mainsheet out to its fullest extent will also help, as will a tight kicking-strap. The Helmsman should also be on the alert to check any tendency to run by the lee, using the rudder as soon as it occurs.

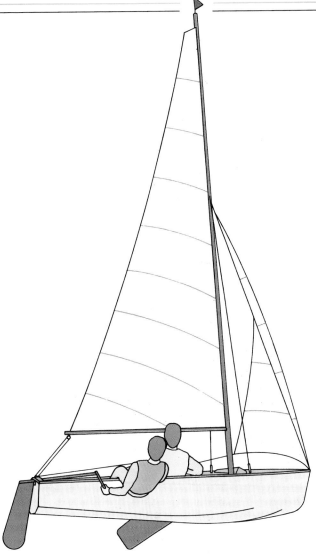

. . . boat broaches, and heels
even more. Only solution
now is to release both
sheets and sit out

Boat is heeling too much.
Crew must sit out and/or
Helmsman must pull the
tiller over, to bear away, or
else . . .

Broaching is the opposite of the problem on the other page, and it is another thing to beware of in strong winds. It occurs if the boat is allowed to heel too much in the normal direction, when sailing with the wind behind. The boat will start to turn towards the wind, leaning over more as it goes, until it is impossible to stop with the rudder. The boom will probably hit the water, pushing the mainsail inwards and making the situation worse as a result. Unless the crew move quickly to balance the boat, a capsize is the most likely outcome.

Once again, the best time to avert broaching is before it has started, by keeping the boat upright. Not letting the mainsheet out enough and having the centreboard down too far may be contributory factors. Broaching may also be encouraged by sitting too far forward in the boat. The same applies to running by the lee. A good rule for the Helmsman in both cases is: *steer the boat under the mast* (i.e. point it in the direction that the mast is leaning).

103

Planing

'Planing' is the term used to describe a moving boat when it rises up in the water and starts skimming across the surface like a surfboard. At the same time there is usually a change in the angle of the boat so that the front is lifted completely clear of the water. There is also a change in the 'wake' (the pattern of waves that a boat leaves on the surface of the water behind it), which becomes broader and flatter than when the boat is moving through the water normally.

Before it will start to plane a boat must reach a certain speed. This varies according to how long the boat is. Large boats have to be moving much faster before they begin to plane than small ones. An ocean liner moves along sedately at 40 kilometres per hour (25 miles per hour), while a speedboat planes furiously at the same speed. The speed at which a particular boat begins to plane is known as its 'maximum hull speed'.

You might expect a boat's speed to increase steadily in proportion to the power of its engine or the force of the wind against its sails, as shown by the yellow line on the graph below. In fact, this is only true of low speeds. What happens next is shown by the orange line on the graph. As the boat begins to approach its maximum hull speed its speed rises much more slowly. This is because it meets with rapidly increasing resistance, caused by large waves which build up at either end.

The only way for a boat to overcome this resistance is by planing. Many boats are effectively unable to plane (including most of more than a few metres long), and these cannot go any faster than their maximum hull speed. When they have reached that speed, even doubling the strength of wind would not make them move any faster. On the other hand, of boats which *are* able to plane (and these include most sailing dinghies), some will do so more readily than others. How easily they plane depends partly on their design and construction, and partly on the skill of the Helmsman and Crew.

Most modern sailing dinghies will plane when the wind is strong enough (about Force 3 or 4). Heavily-built dinghies do not plane so readily, and in some cases not at all, because the amount of force needed to make them sail fast enough is more than the sails can provide, or bear. The same applies to most yachts because of the amount of weight that has to be built into the keel. As a rule, the lighter a dinghy is (and that includes the weight of the crew-members!) the less wind is needed to make it plane.

As well as making sure that a dinghy is light enough, a designer can make it plane more readily by giving it a certain shape under water. Because the front of the boat usually lifts out of the water when the boat is planing, the shape of the forward part does not matter very much. But if the bottom is made broad and flat towards the back, like the bottom of a surfboard, the boat will plane much more easily. This shape is not very streamlined, and at low speeds you should move your weight towards the front of the boat so that the back is not so much in contact with the water. But when it is getting near to its maximum hull speed, streamlining is less important than a flat bottom which helps the boat rise out of the water, so you should move your weight towards the back.

By moving towards the back at the right moment, and in various other ways, you can help a boat to plane. The techniques are described over the page.

Opposite: Planing. The front of the boat rises right out of the water. Note the waves which the boat is making

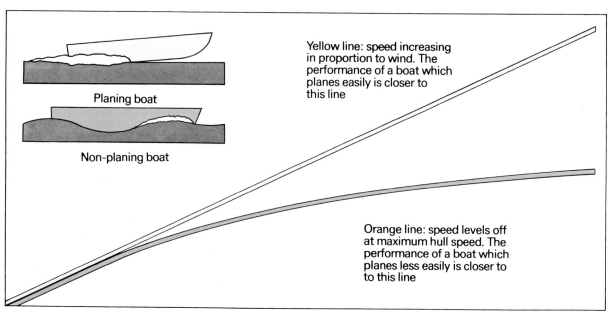

Planing boat

Non-planing boat

Yellow line: speed increasing in proportion to wind. The performance of a boat which planes easily is closer to this line

Orange line: speed levels off at maximum hull speed. The performance of a boat which planes less easily is closer to to this line

Helping the boat to plane

You cannot force a boat to plane if it is not moving fast enough. However, there are various ways of helping it to plane, and making it plane faster.

A sailing dinghy will plane most readily at an angle of, very roughly, 130 degrees to the wind, which is the course on which it sails fastest even when not planing. It takes a stronger wind to make it plane when the wind is directly behind. Only a few, high-performance dinghies can ever plane at an angle of 45 degrees to the wind.

In a strong wind, provided it is sailing at a fairly wide angle to the wind direction, the average dinghy will plane without difficulty. When the wind is less strong it may be on the verge of planing for much of the time, only starting to plane when there is a

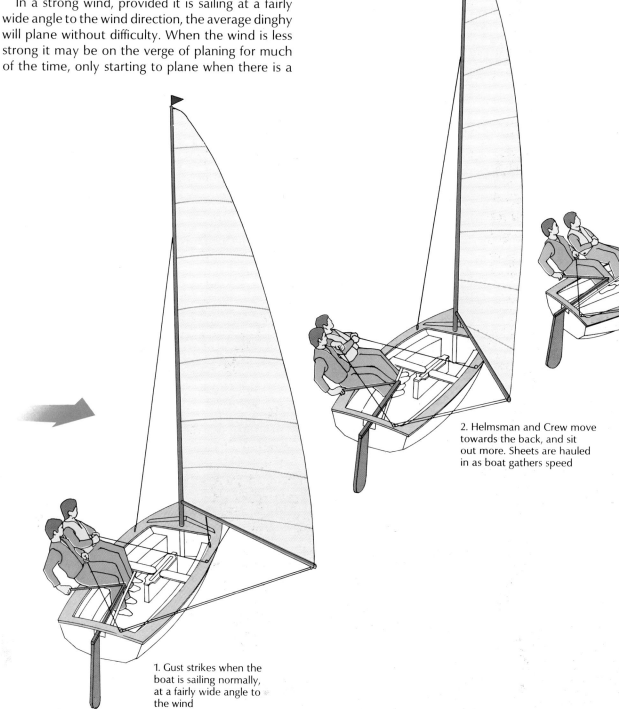

2. Helmsman and Crew move towards the back, and sit out more. Sheets are hauled in as boat gathers speed

1. Gust strikes when the boat is sailing normally, at a fairly wide angle to the wind

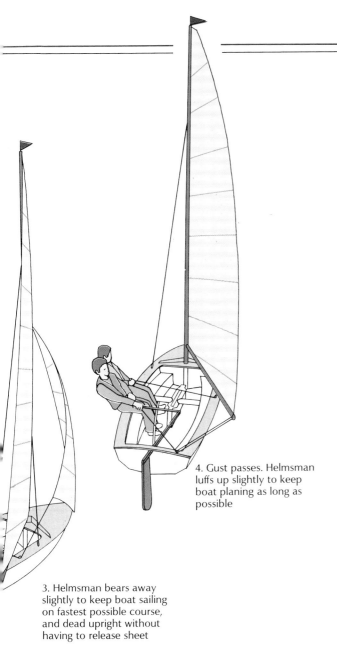

4. Gust passes. Helmsman luffs up slightly to keep boat planing as long as possible

3. Helmsman bears away slightly to keep boat sailing on fastest possible course, and dead upright without having to release sheet

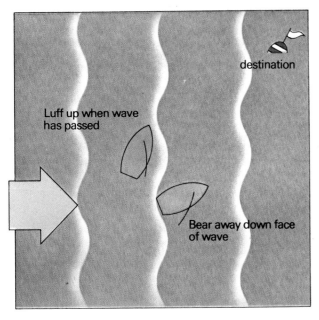

destination

Luff up when wave has passed

Bear away down face of wave

gust. It is under these conditions that skilful handling can make the difference between planing and not planing.

Obviously, anything that makes the boat sail as fast as possible will help it to plane. So part of the technique is simply making sure that the sails are at the correct angle, the centreboard is in the right position, and the boat is completely upright. It is also important that the kicking-strap has been hauled tight (as it should always be in strong winds) so that the mainsail is flat and its whole surface is at the correct angle to the wind. Otherwise, the top part of the sail will twist round so that it is not at the same angle as the bottom half.

When a gust strikes, both crew-members should move nearer to the back of the boat, to lift the front out of the water, at the same time sitting further out, to keep the boat dead upright. You will feel the boat surge forwards as it starts to plane, and if you look behind you you will see the flattened-out wake.

As the boat accelerates, the wind will appear to change direction, so that it is blowing at a narrower angle to the boat's course. This is because the boat creates its own 'wind' as it moves along, and the air that strikes the sails is a combination of that and the real wind. To keep the sails at the correct angle, you should haul in the sheets.

If you were originally sailing at the fastest angle to the wind, the change in the 'apparent wind' will mean that you are no longer on the fastest course. To make the boat plane as fast as possible, the Helmsman should bear away. It is also a good idea to bear away to relieve the pressure on the sails slightly, if you have difficulty keeping the boat dead upright, which is especially important when planing. (If this manoeuvre takes you out of your way, you can easily make up for it when the gust has passed.)

As the gust passes, you may be able to keep the boat planing for a little longer by luffing up again onto the fastest course. In the interval between the wind dropping and the boat losing momentum, the apparent wind will swing round more towards the front of the boat, so the sheets will have to be hauled in further. When the boat has finally stopped planing, move forwards to your original positions.

Waves, if they are big enough, will also help you to plane, rather as if you were surfriding. To get the most benefit from them you should be travelling in more or less the same direction. If your intended destination lies more at an angle to the waves, wait until the crest of a wave is just behind the boat, then bear away so that you go careering down the slope. When the wave finally leaves you behind, you can make up for this 'detour' by sailing more parallel to the crests. (The technique is shown by the two boats in the diagram, both of which are making for the buoy.)

10. Safety and Seamanship

Putting on lifejackets before going afloat in single-handed 'Optimist' dinghies. With a bit of supervision these young sailors can come to little harm if they are wearing lifejackets. These ones are of the 'buoyancy aid' type

Sailing is not a dangerous sport. Almost all accidents can be avoided by taking a few simple precautions. At any time you should be able to ask yourself 'What could I do if things went wrong now?' and get a satisfactory answer. Otherwise, you may be risking your life and the life of anyone who tries to rescue you.

The most common mishap in dinghy sailing is a capsize. This is not a catastrophe. Dinghy racing enthusiasts have been known to capsize several times during the course of one race, and still complete the course. Every dinghy sailor should know how to right his boat when it is capsized. It is a good idea to practise the drill a few times on a safe stretch of water in calm weather, so that you do not have to try it out for the first time under conditions which are not of your own choosing.

If you do capsize accidentally and cannot right the boat for some reason, *stay with it*. You are much safer hanging onto an upturned dinghy than you are alone in the water, and you are much more likely to be seen. Anyone who goes on the water should be able to swim, but you should resist the temptation to try to swim to land from a capsized boat, unless absolutely necessary. The shore is often much further away than it looks across water.

Wearing a lifejacket is even more important than knowing how to swim, wherever you do your sailing. There are various different types. Some are just 'buoyancy aids' which will keep you afloat. Others will hold your face above water even if you are unconscious. When you go sailing you should also be wearing enough warm and waterproof clothing for the conditions, bearing in mind that it is usually a few degrees colder on water than it is on land. If possible there should be someone on shore who knows where you are going and when you should be back. You are safer in company with other small boats, but keep clear of large vessels.

The best and safest course is not always the obvious one, especially if there are tides and currents to contend with. And even on enclosed waters there will be other boats whose actions have to be taken into consideration. The second part of this section is concerned with choosing and planning your course, with reference both to wind and tide conditions, and the movement of other boats.

Righting the boat from a capsize

Capsizing should not hold any fears for the dinghy sailor, and a good crew can get their boat up and sailing again within a couple of minutes, or less. The first thing, however, is to make sure that all the crew-members are safe, and not tangled up with any ropes or sails. While you are in the water you should hold onto the boat so that you do not become separated.

If the boat is on its side, it is usually possible for one crew-member (preferably the heaviest) to lever the boat upright by standing on the centreboard. You can get more leverage by leaning backwards while holding onto the jibsheet. If his weight is not needed, the other person should stay in the water holding onto the front or back of the boat.

If the centreboard was raised when the boat capsized it is usually possible to put your fingers into the slot and pull it out of the bottom of the boat. Otherwise, you can push it from the other side.

The boat should be pointing into the wind when it is upright. So it may be necessary to hold it with the mast just clear of the water while the wind blows it round in the right direction, before completing the righting operation.

When the mast reaches an angle of about 45 degrees the boat will start coming upright of its own accord. This is the moment to start climbing over the side, so that you are inside the boat by the time that the mast is vertical. Sometimes the mast goes too far and the boat capsizes again in the opposite direction. You can prevent this by being inside the boat and able to balance it.

If you want to make sure that the wind will not blow the boat over again as soon as it is righted, you can lower the mainsail before you start. However, with the correct technique, it should be perfectly possible to right the boat with both sails still hoisted.

When the boat has been righted there may or may not be a lot of water inside it, depending on the type of boat. A plastic bucket is the best thing for removing large amounts of water. It is best to scoop it over the side, using a rapid churning motion, rather than filling the bucket to the brim. When most of the water has been removed you can help your companion to get into the boat over the back. The remainder of the water can either be removed with a small bailer as you are sailing along, or, if the boat has 'self-bailers' or 'transom flaps', they will take care of it. (Do not open them until the boat is moving or they will let water in.)

Sometimes a dinghy will turn upside down when it capsizes. To bring the mast up until it is parallel to the water, one crew-member should take hold of the jibsheet, take it over the bottom of the boat, and lean outwards, bracing his feet against the side. If the centreboard is still lowered, or it can be extracted from its slot, the other person should lean backwards holding onto it. Otherwise, he can hold onto the jibsheet with his companion.

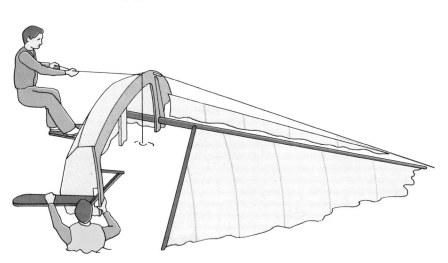

1. Heaviest crew-member stands on the centreboard, holding jibsheet for more leverage. Other person waits, holding onto boat

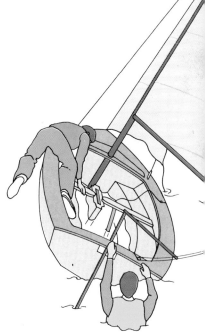

2. Climb into the boat as soon as it starts to come upright of its own accord, and be ready to stop it capsizing again

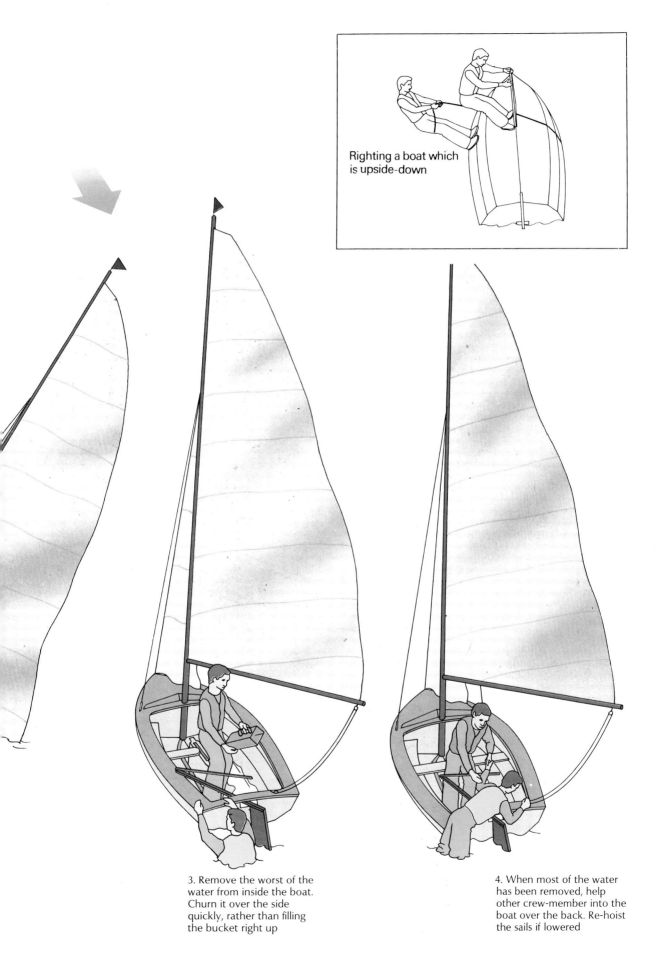

Righting a boat which
is upside-down

3. Remove the worst of the
water from inside the boat.
Churn it over the side
quickly, rather than filling
the bucket right up

4. When most of the water
has been removed, help
other crew-member into the
boat over the back. Re-hoist
the sails if lowered

Making sure the boat floats

All dinghies should have buoyancy chambers of some kind to keep them afloat in the event of a capsize. Most modern dinghies have buoyancy compartments built-in as a matter of course. But it is still wise to check that there is enough buoyancy and that the compartments are watertight. This can be done quite simply by removing the corks from the drain-holes in the back while the boat is tied up against the shore. (Make sure it is tied up properly, in case your doubts turn out to be correct!)

Older dinghies often do not have enough buoyancy, and sometimes have none at all. It is usually a simple enough matter to give a boat extra buoyancy. One of the easiest methods is to install inflated plastic buoyancy bags, which are made in many different shapes and sizes. They must be securely attached to the boat, the usual way being with pieces of webbing passed around the bag and screwed onto the boat at both ends. When the boat is full of water these pieces of webbing must be able to support its weight, and the weight of anyone inside it.

Obviously, buoyancy bags must be fully inflated at all times if they are to have an effect. But they are never quite safe from the danger of being punctured and this consideration, together with the fact that

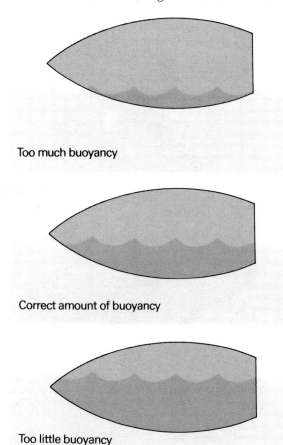

Too much buoyancy

Correct amount of buoyancy

Too little buoyancy

they could become detached from the boat, makes built-in buoyancy compartments preferable. There are usually at least two of these compartments, either one at each end, or else on either side. If there are any openings it is essential to make sure that the covers are in place before you go sailing.

The mere fact that a boat does not sink when it is filled up with water does not mean that it necessarily has enough buoyancy. There must be enough to support the crew-members as well. If a capsized boat sinks below the surface when you try to hold onto it, not only will you be unable to right it, but you will also be left to fend for yourself in the water. When it has been righted, the sides of the boat should be well above water level, even with someone standing inside to bail it out. If the water comes in over the sides it will be impossible to lower the water level inside the boat. Moreover, bear in mind that the surface of the water is not likely to be completely calm when you are trying to do so.

It is also important that the buoyancy chambers are correctly positioned. It is impossible to right a boat if one end is under water while the other one is pointing towards the sky.

The more buoyancy that a boat has, the less water there will be to remove and the easier it will be to remove it. If your boat is fitted with 'self-bailers' or 'transom flaps' (both of which suck water out automatically as it sails along), it may not be necessary to bail by hand at all. If you sail away on the fastest possible course, all the water will probably drain out of its own accord within a few hundred metres. However, automatic bailers only work when the boat is moving fast. If the wind is not very strong or if there is a lot of water on board, you may have to bail some of it out by hand first.

However, it can be dangerous to have too much buoyancy especially at the sides. The problem here is that when the boat is on its side it will float high out of the water, presenting a large surface to the wind. The wind can blow a capsized dinghy along quite fast, often faster than you can swim, so if you get separated from your boat you may not be able to catch it up. If it does not get blown away, a dinghy with too much buoyancy is more likely to turn over completely, which makes it difficult to right. Even if neither of these accidents occur, and the capsized boat stays floating on its side beside you, you may still have difficulty in reaching the centreboard, which will be some distance above your head when you are in the water.

With the correct amount of buoyancy a boat should float half-, or just less than half-, submerged when it is on its side. In this position, it will be comparatively easy to right and to bail dry.

Opposite: Righting a capsized boat. The person standing on the centreboard is holding the jibsheet to get more leverage

Choosing the best course

Sailing is not simply a matter of being able to handle a boat on any course and being able to change from one course to another when you want to. That would only be so if you always sailed in still waters with no other boats or ȯbjects to avoid. But there are times when you have to take more care over choosing your course. And these decisions add more interest to sailing.

One of the things that you should take into account, if you are not sailing in still waters, is the effect of the current. This is not something that you only meet on rivers. In the sea tides do not only rise and fall. The movements of the large bodies of water that cause the tide also create strong currents which usually run parallel to the shore. These tidal currents are most pronounced where the water is forced through a narrow opening, as in an estuary or between islands. Unlike the current of a river, the direction of the flow changes as the tide rises or falls, though not always at exactly the same time as high or low tide. In most parts of the world these changes of direction take place at intervals of approximately six hours. While the current is in the process of changing direction there is normally a period of 'slack water' when the water is motionless.

The size of the difference between high and low tide varies according to the phases of the moon. The largest tides, when the difference is most pronounced, are called 'spring' tides, while the smaller tides are called 'neaps'. The size of the tide makes a difference to the speed of the tidal currents, which are strongest at springs and weakest at neaps.

Before sailing in tidal waters you should find out the times when the current changes on that par-

ticular day and also the strength of the tide in the area where you will be sailing. This information can usually be found in a local newspaper, outside the Harbour Master's office or in a nautical almanac. If you are unfamiliar with the area you will also need to find out the direction in which the current runs, either by looking on a chart or by finding a local person to advise you. (It is often wise to seek local advice about all aspects of a new water.) All this knowledge will help you to plan your sailing expedition for the greatest of safety and the minimum of inconvenience.

On a river where the current always flows in the same direction you will not need to find out all this information before you go sailing. However, the techniques outlined below apply equally to rivers and tidal seas.

Sailing across the current The shortest distance between two points is in a straight line, so a straight course is the shortest. But if you point the boat straight towards a destination which lies across the current, and steer a straight course, you will end up some distance away from your goal. Alternatively, if you keep changing course so that you remain pointing towards it, you will find that you sail a curved course. The correct method is to aim the boat towards a point some distance upstream of where you want to go. The actual course of the boat will then be a straight line to your destination.

A good way to make sure that you are heading in the right direction is to find another fixed object, such as tree or a building, which lies directly behind your target from where you are seeing it. If you steer in such a way as to keep the two objects in line, you should then reach your destination by the shortest possible route.

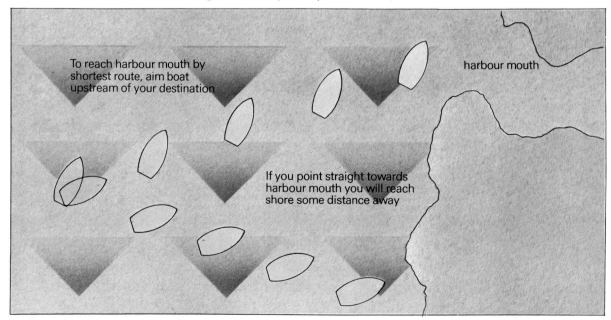

To reach harbour mouth by shortest route, aim boat upstream of your destination

harbour mouth

If you point straight towards harbour mouth you will reach shore some distance away

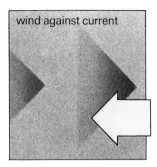

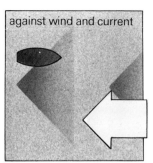

Wind against current This situation does not present the same sort of problem, but if the wind is strong you should beware of the steep waves that build up when there is a fast current running against it.

Against wind and current A sailing boat makes slow progress in this situation. If possible you should sail *upstream* from your starting point, so that you will not have difficulty getting back, unless the tide is going to turn beforehand.

Cheating the current This is one of the most basic techniques of sailing on rivers or tidal waters, and it becomes second nature to people who sail regularly under such conditions. The current is nearly always weakest near the banks of a river or near land, and is stronger in open water. When you are sailing in the same direction as the current, therefore, you will progress faster by keeping out in the strongest part of the flow. When sailing in the other direction, against the current, you will go faster if you keep close to the shore. In both cases, of course, you will not be moving any faster through the water, but you will be moving faster relative to the land. In fact, in very light winds, or when the current against you is very strong, the only way you can make any progress relative to the land may be by keeping near to the shore. However, it is obviously not advisable to sail too close if the water is shallow.

The same rule holds for any wind direction, although it is more difficult to stay close to the shore when you are beating, and you will inevitably have to sail a certain distance out into the current. But you should keep these excursions as short as you can, and do a lot of short zig-zags near to the shore, rather than a few long ones which take you right into the strongest part of the current.

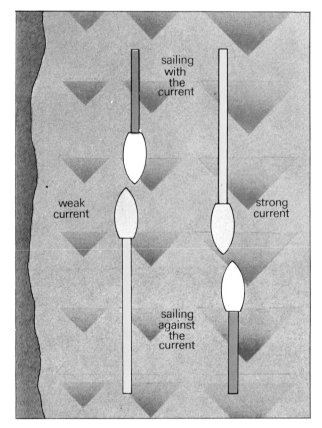

Lee shore This situation and the one that follows are products of the wind direction rather than the current. A 'lee shore' is one which has the wind blowing onto it. In strong winds especially, it is advisable to keep your distance from a lee shore if possible. Waves break with greatest force again against a lee shore, and if something goes wrong you may find that you are unable to prevent yourself being blown onto it.

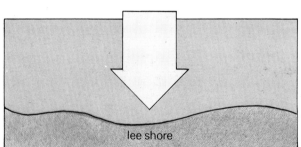

Offshore wind This situation is the opposite of the last one. Care is also needed when the wind is blowing away from the shore, if you are sailing on a large expanse of water or the sea. The water close to land will be relatively calm and sheltered from the wind. But conditions will change as you get further from the shore, and if anything goes wrong the boat will be blown away from land, where the wind may become progressively stronger.

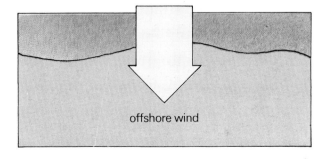

Avoiding other boats

1. Give way to large vessels When a small boat meets a large one which does not have as much freedom of manoeuvre, the small boat should keep out of the way. The 'Power gives way to sail' rule does not apply where the difference in size is very big. For example, between a sailing dinghy and a steamship.

2. Give another boat room to round an obstruction If two boats sailing on parallel courses come to an obstruction, such as a jetty or anchored boat, the boat furthest from the obstruction must allow the other one enough room to round it safely on the inside. If there is more than one boat between you and the obstruction you should allow more room if necessary.

3. Port tack gives way to starboard tack This rule concerns sailing boats only. A boat with its port (left) side nearer to the wind must give way to one with its starboard (right) side nearer to the wind. The rule applies regardless of the course of either boat relative to the wind. They could be meeting head-on. If either boat is sailing with the wind directly behind, then it is on port tack if the mainsail is on the opposite (right) side, and *vice versa*. If your boat is on starboard tack you should steer a straight course while the other boat avoids you. But always be prepared to alter course if a collision seems likely.

4. Windward boat gives way to leeward boat This rule applies to sailing boats which have the same side nearer to the wind. The boat which is sailing at the wider angle to the wind must give way to the other. Once again, if you have right of way you should steer a straight course while the other boat avoids you. If both boats are sailing at the same angle to the wind, but one is coming up behind the other, then the overtaking boat should keep out of the way.

Opposite: Yachts racing in close company. You should keep out of the way of boats racing if you are not taking part yourself

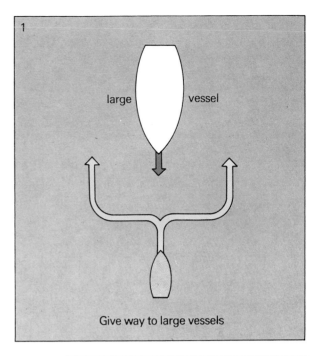

large vessel

Give way to large vessels

Give another boat room to round an obstruction

obstruction

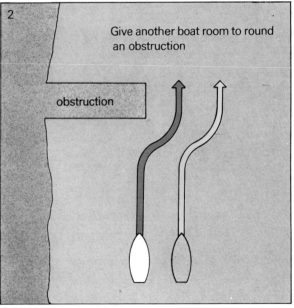

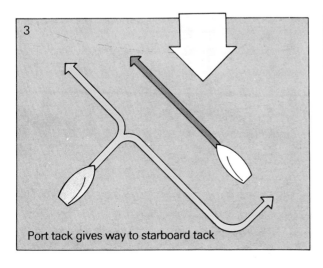

Port tack gives way to starboard tack

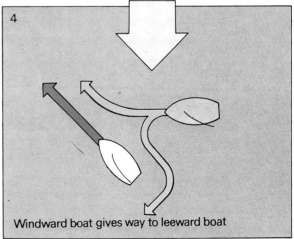

Windward boat gives way to leeward boat

117

Conclusion: Further Horizons

Becalmed. An idyllic moment if you are not in a hurry, but for the crew of this ocean racer, trying to keep their boat sailing as fast as possible in all conditions, it may be a frustrating time

When you have mastered the basic skills in this book, and perhaps some of the more advanced ones, you may want to put them to a particular use. For most people this takes one of two forms, cruising or racing, or you may decide to do a bit of both.

Cruising can mean an expedition lasting a few hours, along a river or a few miles down the coast, or it can mean a voyage to the Caribbean or Greek islands, lasting weeks or more. For the first you would not need more than a large dinghy or small cabin-cruiser, while the second would probably require a fully-fledged yacht with room for several people. In either case you are likely to be sailing a larger boat than the one in which you first started to sail. Initially, you may find it more difficult to manoeuvre than a smaller boat. But all boats are sailed in the same way and it will not take long to get used to it. As well as getting to know a different boat, you will perhaps have to learn something about new aspects of seamanship, like basic navigation, tidal currents or simple weather forecasting. It is partly the variety of skills which makes cruising so attractive.

The racing enthusiast usually spends less time actually on the water than the cruising person, but he or she probably gets more excitement per second. The standard of competition to be found ranges from Olympic level to friendly Sunday afternoon races on a local reservoir. Dinghies usually race on inland waters and sheltered estuaries, while larger yachts may race many miles out at sea. For the newcomer dinghy racing is a good way to start. You will probably need to join a sailing club, which is also a good way to meet more experienced sailors from whom you can learn. Even if you are not dedicated to racing for its own sake, there is no better way to sharpen your reactions and improve your technique than by racing against other boats.

You may not be attracted by either of these alternatives and prefer to take your sailing more gently. Simply being afloat and using the natural power of the wind for propulsion is a pleasure in itself. There are few more satisfying occupations.

Glossary of Nautical terms

A

Aback   State of a sail when the wind is striking it on the wrong side.

Abaft   In the direction of the back of the boat.

Abeam   Level with the beam of the boat (of an object outside the boat).

Aft   Near the back of the boat.

Aloft   Up the mast or rigging.

Amidships   In the middle of the boat.

Apparent wind   The wind as it is actually experienced on a moving boat. It is determined partly by the course and speed of the boat and differs from the true wind in both speed and direction.

Astern   Behind the boat.

Athwartships   Across the boat from side to side.

Awash   Almost submerged, so that the top is level with the surface of the water.

B

Back   (1) To make a sail aback, usually by hauling in the opposite jibsheet to normal. (2) (Of the wind) to change direction anticlockwise.

Ballast   Weight in, or attached to, the bottom of the boat to increase its stability.

Barber hauler   System of ropes for leading the jibsheet further outwards and forwards when sailing at wide angles to the wind.

Batten   Strip of wood, glass-fibre or plastic, which is inserted into the trailing edge of a sail, usually the mainsail, to stiffen it.

Beam   (1) Widest part of a boat's hull. (2) Its width at this point. *On the starboard beam* means level with the boat on the starboard side (of an object outside the boat).

Beam reach   Course of a boat which is sailing with the wind on the beam (i.e. at right-angles to the wind).

Beat   To make progress directly against the wind by sailing at the narrowest possible angle to the wind, with it first on one side then the other.

Bear away   To alter course so that boat is sailing at a wider angle to the wind.

Beaufort Scale   Scale for measuring wind strengths in terms of Forces 1 to 12.

Before the wind   Sailing in the same direction as the wind.

Bend   Name given to certain kinds of knot.

Bermudian rig   Sail plan including a triangular mainsail set on mast and boom only, without a gaff, as is normal on most modern boats.

Berth   (1) Place where a boat can be anchored or moored. (2) Place to sleep on board a boat.

Big boy   Large headsail used in addition to a spinnaker by ocean racers when sailing with the wind behind.

Binnacle   Type of stand in which a compass is mounted.

Bilge   Bottom of a boat, either inside or outside, near the keel.

Block   Pulley wheel, used for sheets, etc.

Boat-hook   Hook mounted on a long handle, for picking up mooring buoys, etc.

Bollard   Wooden or concrete post for attaching mooring ropes.

Bolt-rope   Continuous rope sewn onto the bottom and leading edge of a mainsail.

Boom   Wooden or metal spar to which the bottom of a sail is attached, usually the mainsail.

Boot-top   Stripe painted around the hull at water level.

Bottlescrew   Screw terminal for adjusting the length of a stay.

Bow   Front of the boat. *On the starboard bow* means in front of the boat on the starboard side.

Bowline   Type of knot suitable for making a temporary loop.

Bowsprit   Spar projecting from the front of the boat.

Broach   To slew round involuntarily across the path of the wind when sailing with the wind behind.

Broad reach   Course of a boat which is sailing at a wide angle to the wind direction, but not quite with the wind behind.

Bulkhead   Partition running across the boat from side to side, dividing it into separate compartments.

Bulwark   Side of a ship above the level of the upper deck.

Bumpkin   Spar projecting from the back of the boat.

Buoyancy tank   Closed compartment containing air which keeps the boat afloat when it is full of water. A *Buoyancy bag* serves the same function, but is made of inflatable plastic.

Burgee   Small triangular pennant flown at the top of the mast when not racing.

C

Camber   (1) Convex curve of a boat's deck from side to side. (2) Curve of the surface of a sail.

Cam cleat   Type of jamming cleat with two spring-loaded 'jaws'.

Carvel   Type of wooden boat construction where the longitudinal planks are laid edge to edge.

Cast off   To release the mooring ropes when getting under way.

Cat rig   Sail plan consisting of a mainsail only.

Catamaran   Type of boat with two hulls.

Centreboard   Retractable wooden fin projecting through the bottom of a sailing dinghy to stop it being blown sideways.

Centreplate   Metal centreboard.

Chainplate   Metal plate fixed to the side of the boat as an attachment point for the bottom of the stays.

Chine   Angle formed at the meeting of two planks along the side of a wooden boat of hard-chine construction.

Chinese gybe   Type of gybe, normally accidental, where the bottom of the mainsail ends up on one side of the boat while the top stays on the other. It is prevented by a kicking-strap.

Clam cleat   Type of jamming cleat with grooved sides and no moving parts.

Claw   To work away from the shore against the wind.

Clevis pin   Metal pin used to attach stays, etc.

Cleat   Fitting to which ropes can be attached temporarily.

Clew   Bottom rear corner of a sail.

Clinker   Type of wooden boat construction consisting of longitudinal planks that overlap one another.

Close fetch   Route to a point which can just be reached on one course without having to beat.

Close-hauled   Sailing at a narrow angle to the wind direction.

Close reach   Course of a boat which is sailing at a slightly wider angle to the wind than close-hauled.

Coachroof   Part of a boat's cabin built up above deck level.

Coaming   Raised rim around a cockpit or hatch to prevent water on the deck from entering.

Cockpit   Recess in the deck of a boat where the crew sit and from which it is steered.

Companion or *Companionway*   Steps connecting decks on two levels.

Counter   Underside of the hull where it overhangs the water at the back.

Crew   Second person on a two-person boat besides the Helmsman.

Cringle   Hole in a sail with a rope or metal surround.

Crosstree   Strut projecting from the side of a mast to brace the inner stays.

Cruiser-racer   Yacht designed for both cruising and racing.

Cuddy   Small cabin at the front of a boat.

Cunningham hole   Cringle near the bottom of the luff of a sail through which a control line can be passed to give more tension to the luff when necessary.

D

Dagger-board   Type of centreboard which moves vertically up and down, instead of being pivoted.

Dayboat or *Day-sailer*   Sailing boat of medium size, suitable for short cruises, but without sleeping accommodation.

Dead run   Course of a boat which is sailing with the wind directly behind.

Development class   Class of racing dinghy whose dimensions have to fall within certain limits, stipulated in the rules, but do not have to conform rigidly to one design, allowing the possibility of improvement.

Dinghy   Small open boat which is either sailed or rowed.

Displacement   Weight of a vessel measured by the weight of water displaced by the submerged part of the hull.

Displacement hull   Type of hull which is not designed to plane.

Dodger   Canvas screen attached to the guardrail as a protection from spray.

Doghouse   Part of a boat's cabin raised above the level of the coachroof.

Downhaul   Rope used to hold a spar down.

Downwind   In the same direction as the wind.

Draught   (1) Depth of the hull below water level. (2) Curvature of a sail.

Drop-keel   Metal centreboard which is heavy enough to aid stability.

E

Ebb   State of the tide when it is falling.

Ensign   National flag flown at the back of a boat or at the top of the mizzenmast.

Entry   Forward part of a boat's hull below water level.

F

Fairlead Plastic or metal guide through which a rope is passed.

Fathom A unit for measuring the depth of water equivalent to 1.8 metres (6 feet), or the span of an average man's outstretched arms.

Fender Device, usually made of inflated plastic, which is hung over the side of a boat to prevent damage when it is tied up alongside other boats or a quay.

Fend off To stop a boat hitting another boat or a quay by pushing it away with hands or feet.

Flare Concave curve of a boat's sides so that they overhang the water.

Flood State of the tide when it is rising.

Flush deck Deck of a yacht whose cabin does not rise above deck level.

Foot Lower edge of a sail.

Fore-and-aft Parallel to the longitudinal axis of the boat. A *Fore-and-aft rig* is a sail plan consisting of sails set fore-and-aft.

Foredeck Deck at the front of a boat, in front of the mast.

Foremast Mast standing in front of the mainmast.

Fore-reach To make progress directly into the wind, using momentum built up while sailing normally.

Foresail Headsail set in front of the jib.

Forestay Stay running from the mast to the front of the boat.

Forward In the direction of the front of the boat or near the front of the boat.

Freeboard Distance from water level to the top of a boat's sides.

Fully-battened Description of a sail whose battens extend the whole way from the leach to the luff.

Furl To fold up a sail while it is still attached to the mast, boom or forestay, and tie it in place.

G

Gaff Spar which projects from the mast at an angle and supports the head of the mainsail, seen on some boats with traditional rig.

Galley Area in a cabin set aside for cooking.

Gel coat Smooth outer layer of a glass-fibre hull which contains the colour pigment.

Genoa jib Large jib which stretches back behind the mast.

Go about To tack.

Gooseneck Swivelling joint mounted on the mast which fits into a socket in the end of the boom and attaches it to the mast.

Goosewing To set the jib on the opposite side to the mainsail when sailing with the wind behind.

Ground tackle The equipment which a yacht uses for anchoring or mooring.

GRP Glass resin plastic, known as glass-fibre.

Guardrail Rail or wire running round the side of the boat for safety purposes.

Gudgeon Part of the mounting for the rudder at the back of a dinghy which houses the pintle.

Gunter rig Sail plan including a gaff which projects almost vertically upwards from the mast.

Gunwale Top edge of a boat's sides.

Gybe To swing the sails from one side to the other when changing course with the wind directly behind.

H

Halyard Rope or wire used to hoist a sail or flag.

Hanks Clips fastened onto the luff of the jib for attaching it to the forestay.

Hard-chine Type of wooden boat construction where the longitudinal planks, or plywood sheets, meet at an angle. The resulting shape is often copied in glass-fibre construction.

Harden up To luff up onto a close-hauled course.

Hard over Position of the tiller when it is as far over to one side as possible.

Hatch Opening in a deck or bulkhead.

Head Top corner of a sail.

Head-to-wind State of a boat which is pointing directly into the wind.

Heads Vessel's lavatory.

Headsail Any triangular sail set in front of the mast.

Heave-to To hold a boat stationary. In dinghies this can be done by backing the jib, releasing the main-sheet and pushing the tiller leeward.

Heel (1) To lean over under the pressure of the wind (of a boat). (2) Base of the mast.

Helm A boat's tiller or steering wheel.

Highfield lever Hand-operated lever for rapid ad-justment of the length of a stay.

Hiking Sitting out.

Hitch Name given to certain kinds of knot.

Horse Wire or metal rod on which the mainsheet traveller is mounted on some dinghies, instead of a track.

Hounds Position on the mast at which the stays are attached.

Hull Body of the boat, excluding mast, rigging, etc.

I

Inglefield clip Method of attaching spinnaker sheets, etc., consisting of two interlocking metal rings.

In irons State of a boat which is stationary, pointing directly into the wind and unable to turn in either direction.

In stays In irons.

In stops State of a sail which is furled and tied up in such a way that it can be released immediately.

IOR The International Offshore Rule, the usual system for calculating the handicap 'rating' of an ocean racer.

J

Jamming cleat Quick-release cleat, with or without moving parts.

Jib Triangular sail attached to the forestay.

Jibsheet Rope for controlling the angle of the jib.

K

Kedge Small anchor.

Keel (1) Central timber running the whole length of a wooden boat. (2) Fin projecting downwards from the underside of a yacht's hull to stop it being blown sideways.

Keelson Beam running parallel to the keel on the inside of a boat.

Ketch Type of sailing boat with fore-and-aft sails set on two masts, the smaller one mounted at the back in front of the rudder.

Kicking-strap Rope or wire running diagonally from near the bottom of the mast to a point a short distance along the boom, to prevent the outer end from rising into the air.

Knot Unit of speed equivalent to one nautical mile per hour (1.852 kilometres per hour).

L

Lee Side of an object away from the wind.

Lee helm Tendency of a sailing boat to turn away from the wind.

Lee-ho Instruction to the crew that the boat is tacking.

Lee shore Shore onto which the wind is blowing.

Leech Trailing edge of a sail.

Leech-line Line running down the trailing edge of sail, inside the seam, with which the leech can be tightened.

Leeway Sidewards progress made by a boat when the wind is blowing at an angle to its course.

Leeward Away from the wind, downwind (see diagram).

Level-rating (Of ocean racers) having the same handicap rating. Ocean racers with the same rating can race on the same basis as one-designs.

Lift (Of a sail) to start fluttering when the sheet is too far out or the boat is pointed at too narrow an angle to the wind.

Line squall Short but violent storm of wind and rain, associated with the passing of a cold front.

List (Of a boat) to lean over to one side, for reasons other than the pressure of the wind against the sails (e.g. when it is holed).

Log Instrument for measuring the speed of a boat and the distance travelled through the water.

Luff (1) Leading edge of a sail. (2) To force another boat to luff up, by luffing up when to leeward of it. This is a tactic used when racing.

Luff up To alter course so that the boat is sailing at a narrower angle to the wind.

M

Mainmast Tallest mast of a sailing boat with more than one.

Mainsail Triangular sail set immediately behind the mast.

Mainsheet Rope controlling the angle of the main-sail.

Marina Specially built harbour for yachts.

Mark Usual term for a buoy or other object used as a turning point in the course for racing.

Mast gate Slot at the back of the foredeck to give support to the mast if it is mounted in the bottom of the boat.

Mast ram Device for controlling the amount of bend of a dinghy's mast. It can only be used when the mast is stepped in the bottom of the boat.

Masthead rig Sail plan where the jib is hoisted right to the top of the mast.

Mizzenmast Mast standing behind the mainmast.

Moor   To tie up to a quay, landing-stage or mooring.
Mooring   Permanently laid anchor marked by a buoy, to which a boat can be attached without the need to use its own anchor.
Multihull   Boat with more than one hull.

N

Neaped   State of a boat stranded on a high spring tide, which cannot be refloated until the next series of spring tides.
Neap tides   Series of tides with a small difference between high and low, which alternate with series of spring tides.

O

Ocean racer   Yacht designed for offshore racing.
Officer of the day   Person responsible for organizing races or regattas.
Off the wind   Sailing at a wide angle to the wind.
Offshore wind   Wind blowing away from the shore.
One-design   Sailing boat belonging to a class whose members all conform rigidly to a single design.
On the wind   Sailing at a narrow angle to the wind.
Outhaul   Rope for holding something out (e.g. the clew of the mainsail at the end of the boom).
Overall length   Distance in a straight line between the foremost and rearmost points of a boat's hull.
Overfalls   Steep breaking waves, usually caused by a strong tidal current.

P

Painter   Rope attached to the front of a boat for mooring.
Pay off   (Of a boat) to start turning in either direction, having been pointing directly into the wind.
Peak   Top corner of a gaff mainsail.
Pinch   To point a boat at such a narrow angle to the wind that the sails are flapping continuously, but without bringing it to a complete halt.
Pintle   Part of the mounting for the rudder at the back of a dinghy which fits into the gudgeon.
Pitch   (Of a boat) to have front and back lifted alternately by the waves in rough seas.
Plane   (Of a boat) to skim across the surface of the water at speed, like a surfboard.
Point   To sail at a very narrow angle to the wind, without pinching.

Point of sailing   Course relative to the wind (e.g. close-hauled, broad reach).
Port   Left side, looking towards the front of the boat (see diagram).
Port tack   State of a boat when it is sailing with the wind on the port side (see diagram).
Pound   (Of a boat) to strike waves head-on with jarring force when sailing in rough seas.
Pulpit   Metal framework around the very front of a yacht, for the safety of anyone attaching headsails, dropping the anchor, etc.
Purchase   System of ropes and pulleys which gives the operator a 'mechanical advantage' over whatever he is pulling.

Q

Quarter   Point on the side of the boat roughly midway between beam and stern (see diagram). *On the starboard quarter* means behind the boat on the starboard side (of an object outside the boat).

R

Race   Area of rapid tidal current at certain stages of the tide, often marked by overfalls.
Racing flag   Small square flag flown at the top of the mast when racing.
Rake   Angle of the mast from the vertical, either forwards or backwards.
Rating   Handicap rating of an ocean racer, expressed in feet.
Reach   (1) Any course between close-hauled and a dead run. (2) To sail on such a course.
Ready about   Instruction to a boat's Crew to prepare for tacking.
Reef   To reduce the size of the mainsail by folding or rolling part of it up at the bottom.
Reefing claw   Claw-shaped fitting which fits around the boom on top of a reefed sail, used as an attachment point for the kicking-strap or mainsheet.
Reef point   Short length of thin rope, permanently attached to a sail and projecting on both sides, which is passed around the boom to keep the sail furled when reefed.
Reeve   To thread the end of a rope through a block, fairlead, etc.
Restricted class   Development class.
Ribs   Wooden frames attached at right-angles to the keel to support the side planking.

Rig (1) Arrangement of sails. (2) To prepare a boat for sailing by attaching sails, etc.

Rigging All ropes and wires used for supporting or controlling the mast and sails.

Roach Area of the mainsail created by the convex curve of the leach, usual in terylene or dacron sails.

Rocker Downward curve of the keel.

Roll (Of a boat) To heel alternately to one side then the other when sailing with the wind behind.

Rubbing-strake Strip of wood attached to the side of a boat to prevent it touching other boats or the quay.

Run (1) Course of a boat which is sailing with the wind directly behind. (2) To sail on this course. (3) Rear part of a boat's hull below water level.

Run aground (Of the boat) to hit the bottom in shallow water.

Running rigging Ropes or wires used for controlling the sails.

S

Samson post Post on the deck of a boat for attaching mooring ropes, etc.

Schooner Type of sailing boat with fore-and-aft sails set on two or more masts, the rear one being as tall or taller than the front.

Scupper Opening in the side of the boat to let water drain off the deck or out of the cockpit.

Sea anchor Cone-shaped canvas bag which is lowered into the water to prevent the boat from drifting.

Seacock Tap on a pipe letting water into or out of the boat.

Self-bailer Retractable chute in the bottom of a dinghy which sucks water out as the boat sails along.

Self-draining cockpit Cockpit with a watertight floor raised above water level and scuppers, so that water drains out automatically.

Self-steering gear Equipment attached to a yacht's rudder enabling it to keep itself on one course, essential for single-handed voyages.

Shackle Universal device for attaching sails, sheets, riggings, etc., consisting of a 'U' shape with a removeable bolt.

Sheave Revolving wheel of a pulley block.

Sheer Convex curve of a boat's deck from front to back.

Sheet Rope controlling the angle of a sail.

Shroud Sidestay.

Shy At as narrow an angle to the wind as it is possible to set a spinnaker.

Sidestay Stay running from the mast to the side of the boat.

Sitting out Hanging one's body over the side of the boat to keep it upright.

Skeg Extension to the keel, fitted in front of the rudder on some yachts.

Slip To haul a boat out of the water up a slipway.

Sloop Type of sailing boat with a fore-and-aft mainsail and one jib set on a single mast, like most dinghies and yachts.

Slot Gap between the mainsail and jib.

Snap-shackle Quick-release shackle which can be opened by pressing a button.

Snatch-block Block with a hinged opening so that a rope can be put round or removed without the need to thread or unthread it.

Snub To stop a rope running out by wrapping it around a samson post, winch, etc.

Sole Floor of a cockpit or cabin.

Spars Masts, booms, gaffs, etc.

Spinnaker Large balloon-like sail of light material hoisted on some sailing dinghies and yachts when sailing at a wide angle to the wind.

Spinnaker pole Pole used to hold out the corner of a spinnaker from the mast.

Spitfire jib Small jib made of heavy cloth for use in strong winds.

Splice Method of joining two ropes or wires permanently by weaving their strands together.

Spreader Strut projecting from the side of the mast to brace the stays.

Spring tides Series of tides with a large difference between high and low, which alternate with series of neap tides.

Stanchions Upright posts around the side of the deck which support the guardrail.

Standing rigging All wires supporting the mast.

Starboard Right side, looking towards the front of the boat.

Starboard tack State of a boat when it is sailing with the wind on the starboard side (see diagram).

Stay Wire supporting the mast.

Steerage way Motion through the water, necessary before a boat's rudder can have effect.

Stem Leading edge of a boat's hull.

Step (1) Point on the deck or bottom of the boat where the base of the mast rests. (2) To erect the mast.

Stern Back of the boat.

Stow To put something away.

Suction bailer Self-bailer.

Surf To sail at high speed down the face of a wave when sailing with the wind behind.

Swedish shackle Type of snap-shackle.

Swept deck Flush deck.

T

Tack (1) Bottom front corner of a sail. (2) To change course so that the front of the boat passes through the eye of the wind and the sails cross from one side to the other.

Tang Metal plate fixed to a mast for attaching a stay.

Tender (1) Small rowing dinghy used for rowing to and from a larger boat. (2) Easily heeled.

Thwart Seat running across the middle of a dinghy.

Throat Angle formed by the mast and the gaff in the leading edge of a gaff mainsail.

Tiller Handle for operating the rudder.

Talurit splice Modern method of forming a permanent loop in a piece of wire by enclosing the join with an alloy ferrule and compressing it.

Toe-rail Low rim running round the outside of a yacht's deck.

Toestrap Strap attached to the floor of a dinghy, under which the crew put their feet to support themselves when sitting out.

Topsides Area of a boat's sides which is above the waterline.

Transom Flat stern, seen on dinghies and some yachts.

Transom flap Scupper fitted in the transom of a dinghy, with a non-return flap.

Trapeze Device to enable the Crew of a dinghy to support his entire weight outside the boat to counterbalance the pressure of the wind against the sails. It consists of a wire attached high up on the mast at one end and a harness worn around the Crew's waist at the other.

Traveller Slide which moves along a track or horse, usually as a mobile point of attachment for the mainsheet block.

Trimaran Boat with three hulls.

Trim-tab Small auxiliary rudder mounted at the back of the keel or on the rear edge of the main rudder.

Trysail Small triangular sail made of heavy cloth which is substituted for other sails in severe storms.

Tumble-home Inwards slope of a boat's sides towards the top.

U

Una rig Cat rig.

Uphaul Rope used to hold up a spar.

Upwind In the opposite direction to the wind.

V

Vang Kicking-strap.

Veer (Of the wind) to change direction anti-clockwise.

W

Wake V-shaped pattern of waves made in the water behind a moving boat.

Warps (1) Rope or wire used for mooring. (2) To move a boat in harbour by means of warps.

Waterline length Distance in a straight line between the foremost and rearmost points of a boat's hull at water level.

Way Momentum.

Wear To bring the wind round from one side of a boat to the other by sailing round in a complete circle and tacking, usually to avoid gybing in strong winds.

Weather Side of an object facing towards the wind.

Wetted surface Area of a boat's hull which is in contact with the water. The size of the area has an important bearing on speed, especially in light winds.

Weather helm Tendency of a sailing boat to turn towards the wind.

Weigh To raise an anchor off the bottom.

Whisker-pole Pole used for holding out the clew of the jib when goosewinging.

Winch Revolving drum mounted on deck and operated by handles, around which a rope is wrapped to obtain more leverage when hauling it in.

Windshift Change of wind direction.

Windward Facing the wind, upwind (see diagram).

Y

Yawl Type of sailing boat with fore-and-aft sails set on two masts, the smaller one mounted at the back, behind the rudder.

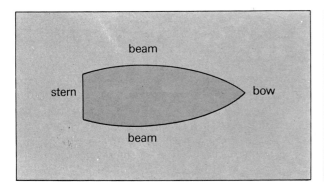

Diagram 1. Parts of the hull. **Bow** and **stern** correspond to 'front' and 'back'. The **beam** is the area around the widest part of the hull, not the whole side of the boat

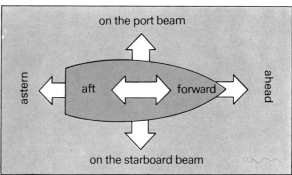

Diagram 3. Directions relative to the boat. **Forward** and **aft** refer to things within the boat, the other terms to objects outside it. **Abeam** can be used for objects on either side

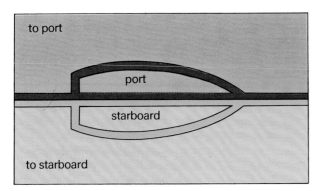

Diagram 2. Sides of the boat. **Port** and **starboard** basically mean 'left' and 'right', but always from the point of view of someone in a boat and looking forwards

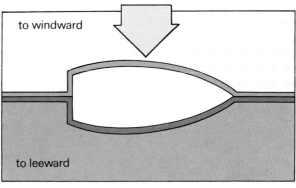

Diagram 4. Directions relative to the wind. The whole area which lies *upwind* is **to windward**. The area which lies *downwind* is **to leeward**

Diagram 5. Courses relative to the wind (points of sailing). These are the terms commonly used to describe the angle at which the boat is sailing. A. **Close-hauled**. B. **Close-reaching**. C. **Beam-reaching**. D. **Broad-reaching**. E. **Running before the wind**. The term **reach** is also used generally to describe any course between close-hauled and running. A boat is said to be on **port tack** or **starboard tack** according to which side the wind is blowing from, regardless of course

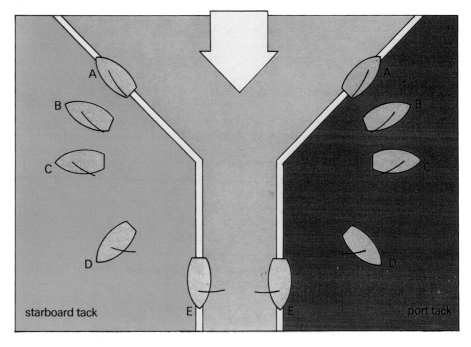

Suggestions for Further Reading

Cruising

Cruising, J.D. Sleightholme (Adlard Coles, London 1963; Granada Publishing Inc, New York 1978)

Cruising Under Sail, Eric Hiscock (Oxford University Press, 1978; Oxford University Press, New York 1965)

Heavy Weather Sailing, K. Adlard Coles (Adlard Coles, London 1967; De Graff, New York 1975)

Racing and boat handling

Basic Windcraft, Alan Watts (David & Charles, Newton Abbot 1976; Dodd Mead, New York 1976)

Sailing Strategy: Wind and Current, Ian Proctor (Adlard Coles, London 1964; De Graff, New York 1977)

Sail Racer, Jack Knights (Adlard Coles, London 1973; Granada Publishing Inc, New York 1977)

Start to Win, Eric Twiname (Adlard Coles, London 1973; Norton & Co, New York 1975)

The Techniques of Small Boat Racing, (Ed) Stuart Walker (Hodder & Stoughton, Sevenoaks 1962; Norton & Co, New York 1961)

Winning, John Oakley (Nautical Publishing Co, Lymington 1972)

Ocean Racing

Ocean Racing and Offshore Yachts, Peter Johnson (Nautical Publishing Co, Lymington 1972; Dodd Mead, New York 1972)

Further Offshore, John Illingworth (Adlard Coles, London 1949)

Amateur boatbuilding

Dinghy Building, Richard Creagh Osborne (Adlard Coles, London 1963; De Graff, New York 1977)

Navigation

Navigation for Yachtsmen, Mary Blewitt (Stanford Maritime, London 1973; McKay, New York 1976)

General seamanship

The Glénans Manual of Sailing (Adlard Coles, London 1967)